Reconceptualizing the Writing Practices of Multilingual Youth

Focusing on adolescent multilingual writing, this text problematizes the traditional boundaries between academic writing in school contexts and self-initiated writing outside of the formal learning environment. By reconceptualizing the nature of adolescent multilingual writing, the author establishes it as an interdisciplinary genre and a key area of inquiry for research and pedagogy.

Organized into six chapters, *Reconceptualizing the Writing Practices of Multilingual Youth* provides an in-depth examination of the writing practices of multilingual youth from sociocultural and social practice perspectives. Drawing on first-hand research conducted with young people, the text questions the traditional dichotomy between academic writing and non-formal equivalents and proposes a symbiotic approach to exploring and cultivating the connections between in- and out-of-school literate lives. By highlighting a bidirectional relationship between formal and informal writing, the text advocates for writing instruction that helps adolescents use writing for entertainment, identity construction, creative expression, personal well-being, and civic engagement, as well as helps them learn to navigate future literacies that we cannot imagine or predict now.

This much-needed text will provide researchers and graduate students with a principled overview and synthesis of adolescent multilingual writing research that is significant yet underexplored in applied linguistics, TESOL, and literacy studies.

Youngjoo Yi is an Associate Professor in Foreign, Second, and Multilingual Language Education at The Ohio State University, United States.

Routledge Research in Literacy Education

This series provides cutting-edge research relating to the teaching and learning of literacy. Volumes provide coverage of a broad range of topics, theories, and issues from around the world, and contribute to developments in the field.

Recent titles in the series include:

Dialogic Literary Argumentation in High School Language Arts Classrooms
A Social Perspective for Teaching, Learning, and Reading Literature
David Bloome, George Newell, Alan Hirvela and Tzu-Jung Lin

Engaging Teachers, Students, and Families in K-6 Writing Instruction
Developing Effective Flipped Writing Pedagogies
Danielle L. DeFauw

Charting an Asian Trajectory for Literacy Education
Connecting Past, Present and Future Literacies
Edited by Chong Su Li

Supporting Student Literacy for the Transition to College
Working with Underrepresented Students in Pre-College Outreach Programs
Shauna Wight

Reconceptualizing the Writing Practices of Multilingual Youth
Towards a Symbiotic Approach to In- and Out-of-School Writing
Youngjoo Yi

For a complete list of titles in this series, please visit www.routledge.com/Routledge-Research-in-Literacy-Education/book-series/RRLIT.

Reconceptualizing the Writing Practices of Multilingual Youth

Towards a Symbiotic Approach to In- and Out-of-School Writing

Youngjoo Yi

Routledge
Taylor & Francis Group

NEW YORK AND LONDON

First published 2021
by Routledge
605 Third Avenue, New York, NY 10158

and by Routledge
2 Park Square, Milton Park, Abingdon, Oxon, OX14 4RN

*Routledge is an imprint of the Taylor & Francis Group, an
informa business*

© 2021 Taylor & Francis

The right of Youngjoo Yi to be identified as author of this work has
been asserted by her in accordance with sections 77 and 78 of the
Copyright, Designs and Patents Act 1988.

Library of Congress Cataloging-in-Publication Data
Names: Yi, Youngjoo, author.
Title: Reconceptualizing the writing practices of multilingual youth :
    towards a symbiotic approach to in-and out-of-school writing /
    Youngjoo Yi.
Description: First Edition. | New York : Routledge, 2021. | Series:
    Routledge research in literacy education | Includes bibliographical
    references and index.
Identifiers: LCCN 2021001605 (print) | LCCN 2021001606 (ebook) |
    ISBN 9780367417758 (Hardback) | ISBN 9780367816223 (eBook)
Subjects: LCSH: Linguistic minorities–Education–United States. |
    Language arts (Middle school)–United States. | Language arts
    (Secondary)–United States. | Composition (Language arts)–Study
    and teaching (Middle school)–United States. | Composition
    (Language arts)–Study and teaching (Secondary)–United States. |
    Written communication–Social aspects–United States. | Multilingual
    persons–Social conditions. | Language arts teachers–In-service
    training–United States.
Classification: LCC LC3731.Y52 2021 (print) | LCC LC3731 (ebook) |
    DDC 372.6/044–dc23
LC record available at https://lccn.loc.gov/2021001605
LC ebook record available at https://lccn.loc.gov/2021001606

ISBN: 978-0-367-41775-8 (hbk)
ISBN: 978-1-032-03543-7 (pbk)
ISBN: 978-0-367-81622-3 (ebk)

Typeset in Times New Roman
by KnowledgeWorks Global Ltd.

Dedicated to Grace and Minwoo

Contents

Author Bio

Youngjoo Yi is an Associate Professor in Foreign, Second, and Multilingual Language Education in the College of Education and Human Ecology at the Ohio State University, United States. She is co-editor of *TESOL Journal* (2019–2022), guest-edited a special issue on multimodal composing for the *Journal of Second Language Writing* (2020), and co-edited a volume on multimodal writing from multilingual perspectives (Springer, 2021). Yi's teaching has revolved around middle and secondary students' English language learning in the United States and Asia, K-16 world/heritage language instruction, and graduate-level courses in TESOL and literacy education. As an applied linguist and qualitative researcher, her research centers on the language and literacy experiences of multilingual students and their identity construction. Drawing from sociocultural perspectives of language and literacy learning, her work has explored how adolescent multilingual students engage in multilingual, digital, and multimodal literacy learning across various contexts and negotiate their identities through multiple language and literacy practices. Her research has been published in various journals, including *Applied Linguistics, CALICO Journal, Canadian Modern Language Review, Foreign Language Annals, Journal of Adolescent and Adult Literacy, Journal of Second Language Writing, TESOL Journal, TESOL Quarterly*, and others.

Acknowledgments

This book is the result of many years of researching, teaching, thinking, and talking about adolescent multilingual writing with numerous people. This book owes its existence to them. First and foremost, I am deeply appreciative of many adolescent multilingual students, particularly those who have shared their literate lives with me, taught me what's like to be adolescent multilingual students, and helped me broaden my perspectives of language, literacy, and learning. For me, adolescent multilingual students have been the most intriguing group of students to work with and for, and they have helped me stay curious about language learning and teaching. I have been privileged to research and write about them.

In addition, this book could not have been done if other colleagues, students, and friends had not generously provided support, inspiration, encouragement, and advice. Specifically, I would like to thank, Alex Mikhail, Dong-shin Shin, Eun Jeong Park, Kun Chen, and Seonhee Cho, for their critical feedback on my chapter drafts. When I asked for their help, it was the busiest and craziest time of the semester. Yet, they all graciously offered me insightful commentary and showed their confidence in me as a scholar and writer, which enabled me to stay focused and finish this book.

I would also like to express my heartfelt gratitude to the mentors who initially encouraged me to pursue a book project on adolescent multilingual writing and read some of the earliest drafts, including Alan Hirvela and Diane Belcher. I am also especially grateful to the Department of Teaching & Learning and the College of Education and Human Ecology at the Ohio State University for their support, especially for granting a research leave during the COVID-19 pandemic. I was able to concentrate on and complete this book project during my research leave. I also thank to the reviewers of the book proposal and the manuscript, as well as Ellie Wright and other members at Routledge.

And above all, I offer unbounded gratitude to the two people I love the most – my daughter, Grace, and my husband, Minwoo – as well as my parents and in-laws in Korea, for their encouragement, forbearance, and support. Most of the actual writing of this book was done during the COVID-19 pandemic. Three of us and our Golden retriever Kay have been staying at home for 11 months so far (as of January 2021). During this long stay-at-home period, Grace, my 5-year-old daughter, had to learn to play on her own, and my husband had to embrace so many quiet nights alone while I was rushing to meet the deadlines. Were it not for their patience and understanding, this book would not have been possible.

1 An Introduction to Adolescent Multilingual Writing

Entering the Conversation

Adolescent multilingual students (e.g., immigrant, refugee, and English language learning youth) engage in wide-ranging texts and textual practices in their daily lives. For instance, they write persuasive five-paragraph essays on topics selected or assigned, create PowerPoint slides for class presentations, exchange instant text messages with their peers, make *How to make* videos to upload to their social networking sites, keep diaries or journals, and engage in family literacy required in the everyday lives of immigrants (e.g., completing medical forms or documents). Through these various kinds of writing, many adolescent multilingual students fulfill school requirements, express their ideas and feelings, explore the meaning of personal and social issues, record lived experiences, entertain themselves or others, negotiate multiple identities, and seek out or share information in the language (English) they are still learning. As such, their writing practices are deeply embedded in their lives. Yet, they may not realize it or do not think of writing as an important part of their everyday lives.

Although writing is everywhere in adolescent multilinguals' daily lives, their writing experience and development drastically vary, which causes great challenges for understanding and teaching them. For instance, Soohee, a 9th grade English learner (EL) from South Korea, took an intermediate English as a Second Language (ESL) class in her first semester in an American high school. Later in her third and fourth semesters, she took a Creative Writing class as an elective course and an Honors English, respectively, and successfully passed both classes. On the other hand, Hoon, an 11th grade EL, repeated an advanced ESL class three times and never exited from the ESL program. Surprisingly, even though he repeated the ESL class three times, he managed to maintain a 3.4 (out of 4.0) grade-point average and constructed an academic achiever identity, while simultaneously struggling with his stigmatized ESL student identity. Differing from Hoon's case, Yeseong, a 10th grade multilingual writer, extensively engaged in meaningful and critical writing activities in informal settings, such as pen-pal exchanges with teens overseas and emails to the Korean Culture Center in the Embassy of the Republic of Korea in the United States to request some artefacts she could share at the Korean Culture Club at her school. Yet, she had constantly struggled with academic achievement and academic writing, which caused huge conflicts with her immigrant parents. All three students came to the United States from the same home country (South Korea) during their adolescence, shared the same first language with varying degrees of Korean literacy, and attended high schools with similar demographics and ratings that were located in suburban areas in the Midwestern United States. As such, despite similar backgrounds, writing experiences for adolescent multilingual students can differ from one student to another.

With such rich and diverse writing engagement, adolescent multilingual students are arguably the group that experiences the most *tension* and *contradiction* between in-school and out-of-school writing practices. At least in the context of the United States, adolescent multilingual students are often asked to engage in narrowly-defined and standards-driven writing activities in the classroom (Enright & Wong, 2018). In other words, "writing practice in many [American] secondary schools is becoming less frequent, more prescriptive, and more limited in terms of genres and purposes for writing" (Ortmeier-Hooper & Enright, 2011, p. 174). One of the reasons for this phenomenon is that teachers feel the urgent need to help students pass high-stakes tests so that students will be able to receive a high school diploma and enter college. Some teachers may teach writing to the test, emphasizing a few genres that typically appear on it (e.g., expository and persuasive essays). As a result, students are likely introduced to "narrow restrictive norms for academic writing, with the most restrictive norms occurring in the classes" (Enright & Gilliland, 2011, p. 182). Anecdotally, I have observed a teacher who explicitly taught ELs that "An argumentative essay needs to have five paragraphs, and each paragraph needs to have five sentences," and ELs who worried after their high-stakes writing tests because they wrote only four paragraphs, not five.

On the contrary, when adolescent multilingual students choose to write outside of school, they tend to use multiple languages (e.g., their first, second, third languages, and mixture of all), semiotic resources (e.g., drawings, signs, and background music), and mediums (print-based and digitally-mediated) to voluntarily engage in a wider range of writing activities. Emerging technologies enable them to experience an ever-widening range of writing practices in their daily lives, such as writing fanfiction in an online community (Black, 2008; Jwa, 2012), writing and interacting with social networking sites (Hughes & Morrison, 2014; Vanek, King, & Bigelow, 2018), communicating via instant messaging (Lam, 2004), and creating digital stories (Yi, Kao, & Kang, 2017). Thus, both teachers and students may experience a discrepancy between the narrow focus on academic writing and the wide range of writing activities in which students engage outside of school. As a result, students experience tensions in writing practices between in-school and out-of-school contexts. Such tensions themselves may not be the issue, but rather the problem may lie in how we conceptualize adolescent multilingual writing and how we understand the relationships and boundaries[1] between academic writing in school and self-initiated, voluntary writing outside of school (e.g., at home or in the community).

Given the changing landscape of literacy in adolescent multilingual students' everyday lives and the increasing tensions between in-school and out-of-school writing practices, I aim to reconceptualize adolescent multilingual writing in and outside of school in this book, from a sociocultural view of literacy, by (a) exploring both in-school and out-of-school writing in a comprehensive manner, (b) critically examining blurred boundaries between in-school and out-of-school writing, and (c) employing a *symbiotic approach* (considering a two-way, symbiotic relationship between in-school and out-of-school literate lives) to understand and promote adolescent literacy.

The symbiotic approach that I propose in this book refers to a practice and a principle of examining and cultivating a mutually beneficial, bi-directional relationship between in-school and out-of-school literate lives. This symbiotic approach highlights the importance of exploring the bi-directional relationship between in-school and out-of-school writing practices, while paying greater attention to how school writing experiences, practices, and knowledge impact students' out-of-school literate lives and vice versa. As Perkins (2009) powerfully pointed out, "The whole point of education is to prepare for *other times* and *other places*, not just to get better in the classroom" (p. 12) (emphasis added). In that regard, writing practices and instruction in the classroom should help adolescent multilingual writers successfully use writing for personal well-being, entertainment, civic engagement, and more beyond regular school hours. Furthermore, writing practices in school should help our students learn how to navigate future literacy practices that we cannot even imagine or predict.

Similarly, researchers in the fields of applied linguistics and Teaching English to Speakers of Other Languages (TESOL) have examined and called for bridging out-of-school writing experiences and classroom practices (Daniel, 2018; Li, 2012; McCarthey, 1997; Orellana & Reynolds, 2008; Wiltse, 2015). Yet, out-of-school writing has mostly been conceptualized as resources *for* academic writing, which is somewhat limited because it suggests that out-of-school writing practices are less significant and legitimate than in-school writing. Through this narrow perspective, out-of-school writing has been seen as secondary or supplementary to in-school, academic writing. In comparison, the symbiotic approach proposed in this book provides researchers and practitioners with a more expanded and critical view of adolescent multilingual writing and adolescent literacy by allowing them to explore a bi-directional relationship between in-school and out-of-school writing.

Key Issues in Adolescent Multilingual Writing Research and Pedagogy

As readers can imagine, many adolescent multilingual students in English-medium instructional settings face multiple academic challenges, including challenges with academic writing. They need to learn English as an additional language, gain content area knowledge in their second language (L2), manage high-stakes standardized tests that are designed for native English-speaking peers, and develop academic literacies in their L2 while still developing their first language (L1) literacy. Particularly with academic writing, they additionally face "cognitive, linguistic, communicative, contextual, textual and affective constraints common to all writers" (Olson, Scarcella & Matuchniak, 2015, p. 9). In other words, when adolescent multilingual students write in their L2, they are cognitively overloaded, feel challenged to gain and use their language knowledge and experiences (e.g., figuring out how to spell a word and construct a sentence, where to place an adverb, how to introduce a topic, and how to use a specific language feature), and need to learn how to write for a specific audience and purpose and in a variety of genres. Furthermore, they may lack cultural knowledge and experiences required to write about a certain topic (e.g., Halloween, Thanksgiving dinner). Many adolescent multilingual writers juggle all these constraints as they write in an L2.

Not surprisingly, recent data has shown that adolescent multilingual students, especially adolescent ELs tend to poorly perform on high-stakes testing compared to their non-EL (English-speaking) peers and are not adequately prepared to meet the writing demands of school and career (Enright, 2010; Faggella-Luby, Ware, & Capozzoli, 2009). For example in the United States, according to the 2011 National Assessment of Educational Progress (NAEP) report (the latest report available as of December, 2020[2]), writing by 8th grade ELs was scored 44 points (out of 300) lower on average than their non-EL counterparts' writing. This discrepancy grew to 56 points when they reached the 12th grade. Furthermore, only 20% of 12th grade ELs performed at or above the *Basic* level for writing, whereas 80% of their non-EL counterparts achieved the same, *Basic* level, and only 1 percent of 12th grade ELs performed at or above the *Proficient* level (NAEP results are reported as percentages of students performing at the *Basic, Proficient, and Advanced* levels) (National Center for Education Statistics, 2012).

The challenges that adolescent multilingual students face and the corroborating writing assessment data as mentioned above have drawn researchers' and practitioners' attention to issues in writing pedagogy for adolescent multilingual writers. In the context of the United States, writing instruction is typically integrated into the English Language Arts curriculum where other curricular priorities and pressures (e.g., critical reading and literary analysis) are often emphasized rather than explicit writing instruction (Ortmeier-Hooper & Enright, 2011). In addition, rigid standards and high-stakes testing have greatly influenced writing instruction (e.g., teaching to test). A variety of forms of writing in which students engage everyday (e.g., informal, voluntary writing activities) are not well-regarded or acknowledged in school settings.

Along with a narrow range of writing activities in classrooms, many adolescent multilingual students' limited exposure to school-valued writing genres is another concern. Based on a two-year study of middle school students of Latino background in the United States, Valdés (1999) pointed out that "As opposed to English monolingual students who have been surrounded by texts of different kinds all of their lives, ESL students had limited exposure to the traditions of written edited English" (p. 174). This observation was reported approximately 20 years ago; however, not much has changed over the years. This may be because many teachers of ELs may fear engaging their students with analytical essay writing since they believe that analytical writing can be too complex or sophisticated for ELs of limited proficiency (Yi, Kao, & Kang, 2018).

Proper teacher preparation for writing instruction seems to be another related issue. Many middle and high school teachers (including EL teachers) feel that they are poorly prepared to teach writing in their context. In other words, many teachers may feel that they have not had sufficient education on (L2) writing instruction during their teacher education program or through professional development (National Commission on Writing in America's Schools and Colleges, 2003). Furthermore, some teachers may not view writing as their responsibility (Applebee & Langer, 2011; Kiuhara, Graham, & Hawken, 2009). Overall, relative lack of teacher education or professional development about writing pedagogy seems to lead to challenges for both teachers and students in the classroom.

In terms of research, there is a huge void of research for adolescent multilingual writers (Cumming, 2012; de Oliveira & Silva, 2013; Graham, Early, & Wilcox 2014; Harklau & Pinnow, 2008; Leki, Cumming, & Silva, 2008; Perin, de la Paz, Piantedosi, & Peercy, 2017). Historically, L2 writing research has responded to the urgent need to help a great number of international *college students* with their academic success in English-medium instructional settings (Matsuda, 2003). Thus, adolescent multilingual writing research has lagged far behind post-secondary L2 writing research. In the L1 writing and literacy scholarship that has influenced L2 writing research, adolescent writers have largely been neglected (Graham & Perin, 2007; Tate, Warschauer, & Kim, 2019) in favor of writing and literacy development of young children or college students. In particular, early literacy research has always been the central focus of literacy research. For instance, early reading research has been given a priority by most of the federal agencies that have funded educational research, while writing research has not been funded comparatively. Worst yet, adolescent multilingual writing research has not even been on the radar of funding agencies.

All these issues in adolescent multilingual writing pedagogy and research briefly stated above require a collective effort among researchers, teacher educators, and classroom teachers to address them. That is, teaching writing to adolescent multilingual students should be a shared responsibility, which is something that I try to address in this book. EL teachers and content area teachers need to work together to provide a writing curriculum, and researchers and teacher educators should address writing pedagogy in teacher education. One promising aspect of teacher education in terms of writing pedagogy is that teacher education programs seem to introduce pre-service teachers to expanded notions of writing and the multiplicity of writing and literacies rather than a singular academic literacy and writing (Enright, 2010). Yet, we still need more discussion around writing pedagogy, especially "research-based" instruction (Graham & Perin, 2007) in teacher education.

Adolescent Multilingual Students: Various Backgrounds

Although I use a term, *adolescent multilingual students* in this book, there is a great diversity within this student population, particularly in terms of their language and literacy profile. For instance, some students are newly arrived ELs with strong or weak first language (L1) writing competence; others are often labeled as Long-Term English Learners (LTELs) with various levels of L2 writing competence. Further, no single term or label is adequate to identify adolescent multilingual students in terms of their strengths, needs, and challenges. While I am aware of the problematic nature of categories or labels (Kibler & Valdés, 2016; Kohls, 2018), I still use some of these widely-recognized categories or labels (e.g., L2, bilingual, refugee, long-term ELs) with caution because they are often useful in both research and teaching (Goodwin & Jiménez, 2019). By making a cautionary note here, I would like my audience to be more critical and conscious about possible issues that arise from using such categories or labels since they may impact the individuals described with such terms. In the subsequent sections, I explain several sub-groups of adolescent multilingual writers (e.g., newcomers, long-term ELs, refugee students, and international students). These subgroups of students share some common characteristics to varying degrees; yet, it is critical to understand that the needs and responsibilities of these subgroups could vary.

Long-term English Learners versus Newcomers

Depending on how long adolescent multilingual students have stayed in the school system and received ESL services, they can be divided into LTELs and newcomers. Long-term ELs tend to have most of their formal schooling in the host country (e.g., Australia, Canada, the United States), yet still have not reached the criteria for reclassification as fluent in English. Some call them "Long-Term English Learners (LTEL)" (Clark-Gareca, Short, Lukes, & Sharp-Ross, 2020; Olsen, 2010), and others call them "Generation 1.5 immigrants" or "US-educated multilingual writers" in the US context (Roberge, Losey, & Wald, 2015). Many of the LTELs speak English quite fluently and are familiar with the host culture; however, their academic skills are often considered below grade level and so they often encounter challenges with academic literacy tasks (Bunch 2006; Souryasack & Lee, 2007). Their academic writing often demonstrates some errors that ELs make as well as those made by remedial native-English-speaking peers. In fact, many long-term ELs have called the host country home because many of them were born in the host country or have lived in the host country long enough to call it home. For instance, "57 percent of adolescent learners classified as limited English proficient were born within US borders and thus are second- or third-generation residents" (Rance-Roney, 2010, p. 33). More recently, the Census Bureau's 2016 American Community Survey estimated that among public school students ages 5–17 who reported speaking English "less than very well," 72% were born in the United States (Bialik, Scheller, & Walker, 2018).

Newcomers, as the term indicates, are those who recently arrived in a host country (Martin & Suárez-Orozco, 2018). Some attend newcomer schools, consisting entirely of recently arrived ELs, that are designed to provide newcomers with special support for the academic, cultural, and socio-emotional challenges in a new country for a limited period of time before enrollment in regular ESL programs or content area classrooms (e.g., Scully, 2016). Others attend regular schools while receiving an ESL service (as seen in Fránquiz and Salinas, 2011). Recently, Allard (2016) termed older newcomers who matriculate relatively late in the school year, *latecomers*, to highlight unique challenges for newcomers who have limited time to learn the language and pass required tests to graduate high school. Within a continuum of long-term ELs and newcomers, we see several groups of students (e.g., refugee, transnational, or international students). The subsequent sections explain them with quite distinctive characteristics of their own.

Refugee Students

Refugees are typically people who have been forced to leave their countries due to wars or great social difficulties (e.g., violence, persecution, oppression, natural disaster), unlike students who voluntarily choose to move. Many refugee adolescents have no, little, or severely interrupted formal schooling with very limited L1 literacy or no literacy skills in any language. Refugee students with limited or interrupted formal education face unique challenges (e.g., figuring out school organizational structures and classroom routines) as compared to immigrant or international students with strong educational backgrounds (Faltis & Valdés, 2010; Harushimana, 2011; McBrien, 2005). When resettling in a new country, learning a new language, and attending school, they often need not only academic, but also psychological and emotional support in school. Recently, refugee students have been considered as a distinctive sub-group of ELs because refugees are as diverse as any other groups of multilingual students, and some challenges are very particular to refugee students. With the increasing attention to this particular group of students, a growing number of studies have documented their language and literacy learning experiences (Daniel, 2018; Karam, 2018; Ortmeier-Hooper, 2013; Shapiro & Farrelly, & Curry, 2018; Stewart, 2015), and there has been a Refugee Concerns Interest Section (RCIS) in the international organization of TESOL. In addition, a new term *Students with Interrupted Formal Education* (SIFE) has been more widely used to recognize the special needs of this particular group of students.

Transnational (Immigrant) Students

Transnational youth are another emerging group of adolescent multilingual students. They tend to live across national, geographic borders, often traveling back and forth between a home and host country. They make two-way movements in terms of their access to resources and capital, in addition to the flow of locations and commodities they experience (Yi, 2009). They typically cultivate continuous transnational and transcultural ties to their home country while possessing a "dual frame of reference" (Louie, 2006, p. 363) or "bifocality" (Vertovec, 2004, p. 974) in order to "explore or evaluate their life experiences and outcomes within their host country" (Yi, 2009, p. 101). With more advanced technologies and globalization, these students' transnational lived experiences tend to allow them to engage unique options and opportunities for literacy learning and identity construction, which is further elaborated in Chapter 3 (Jiménez, Smith, & Teague, 2009; Lam & Warriner, 2012; McGinnis, Goodstein-Stolzenbrg, & Saliani, 2007; Sánchez & Kasum, 2012; Skerrett, 2012; Yi, 2009).

International Students

In addition to refugee and transnational (immigrant) students, there is a slowly growing number of international students in middle and high schools in English-medium instructional settings. Traditionally, we have seen a great number of international students at the tertiary level, but we now have an increasing number of secondary international students in the classrooms in Anglophone countries like Australia, Canada, the United Kingdom, and the United States (Popadiuk, 2010; Rahimi, Halse, & Blackmore, 2017). Some are study-abroad exchange students (Sauer & Ellis, 2019; Sustarsic, 2020) and others are temporarily transferred to English-speaking countries because of familial relocation. While some international adolescents seek higher education in an English-speaking host country, many of them are also preparing for their reintegration into the educational system in their home country in the near future and have a bi-focal attention to academics. In other words, doing well in a host country and being prepared for their re-entry into the educational system in their home country are equally important to them; thus, these international students are likely to engage in writing and literacy practices in both languages (e.g., Haneda & Monobe, 2009).

Finally, I need to reiterate that although I introduce several terms indicating subgroups of adolescent multilingual students, some definitely overlap. For instance, an international student who just arrived in a host country is considered a newcomer student, and simultaneously he or she can be a transnational student while engaging in transnational daily activities (e.g., constantly reading about issues in home and host countries and communicating with people across home and host countries).

Unpacking Terms: Adolescent Multilingual Writing

Before moving onto discussing the nature of adolescent multilingual writing in this book, I unpack such terms as *adolescent, multilingual,* and *writing.* None of the three words is a "simple, unified, unproblematic term" (Christenbury, Bomber, & Smagorinsky, 2010, p. 3). Thus, it is critical to unpack them first.

Adolescence

The term, adolescence is derived from the Latin word *adolescenre,* meaning "grow up" or "grow from childhood to maturity" (Lerner & Steinberg, 2009). Although the World Health Organization (WHO) defines an adolescent as anybody between ages 10 and 19, the term is more complex. The most familiar and dominant view of adolescence is that adolescence is a distinctive and unique phase of human life, in which one undergoes physical, biological, psychological, and emotional change. On the other hand, educational researchers began to problematize a typical construction of adolescence that framed it from a deficit perspective and called for a re-thinking of the concept (Lesko, 2012; Sarigianides, Lewis, & Petrone, 2015). Viewing adolescence as a sociocultural construct, these scholars argue that "adolescence is not fixed, nor stable, nor tethered to the will of body. What we expect of adolescence and adolescents fluctuates with contexts and circumstances" (Sarigianides, Lewis, & Petrone, 2015, p. 15). In addition, adolescents are "people with *agency* and *expertise*, though how this manifests itself may vary significantly across contexts and situations" (Clark, Blackburn, & Newell, 2010, p. 117) (emphasis added). In this book, I am more aligned with this sociocultural view of adolescence and adolescents and hope that when the readers read, think about, and discuss adolescent multilingual users and writers, they should view the changes that adolescents are experiencing as developmental, fluid yet resourceful.

Adolescence is also a time when students are seeking to learn about who they are, who they do (not) want to be, how they want to express themselves to the world, and how they position themselves in relation to others, among others. Adolescent multilingual students, like all teens, are likely to struggle to develop social identity, self-esteem, and resilience. They can use writing to express and explore new identities, to position themselves in new ways, and to understand the shifting perspectives in their lives while exploiting a variety of linguistic, textual, and cultural resources available to them (Cox, Jordan, Ortmeier-Hooper, & Schwartz, 2013; Taylor & Cummins, 2011; Yi, 2009). Reportedly, the issue of identity negotiation through writing is more complicated for multilingual adolescents (Yi, 2010). For these students, the first language is likely to represent a very significant part of who they are. As they struggle to learn how to express themselves in their new language (English), they are likely to feel frustrated by their incapability to fully express themselves in a meaningful and satisfying manner. Consequently, many of these students need more than one language to fully express themselves. While mentioning their challenges with writing in their second language (L2), I also need to acknowledge that writing in L2 can be "a powerfully motivating and potentially transformative force" (Vollmer, 2002, p. 3) for some adolescent multilingual students as they take advantage of opportunities to communicate a sense of themselves and understand their linguistic and cultural writing resources. As such, writing can provide a powerful tool to negotiate the identities of multilingual students during adolescence.

Multilingual

In this book, I decide to use *multilingual* and *multilingual students* rather than second language (L2) and L2 writers for several reasons. First, this comprehensive term, multilingual students, can encompass widely divergent linguistic and cultural backgrounds of adolescents and reflect the heterogeneity of the students. The term, multilingual, is meant to signify an important part of the diversity of writers who negotiate multiple linguistic and cultural repertoires and identities. Second, terms, like ESL, limited English proficient (LEP) or bilingual (at least in the US context) often represent a negative marker or status in school and society. Thus, by using the term, multilingual, I challenge deficit perspectives of ELs and promote an ideology that multilingual (including bilingual and ESL) backgrounds are assets and positive markers for our students who are often linguistically-talented. Finally, labels, like ESL, are often not accurate when describing multilingual students who learn and use English as their third or fourth language in their lives.

Writing

I use a term, *writing* over *literacy* for several reasons. First, this book is about writing. Second, when researchers and practitioners use the word, literacy, it seems to automatically refer to and/or emphasize reading over writing. That is why scholars have pointed out that writing has been considered a "neglected R" among three Rs (reading, writing, and arithmetic) (Mo et al., 2014; National Commission on Writing in America's Schools and Colleges, 2003; Sessions, Kang, & Womack, 2016). In addition, I often call adolescent multilingual students *adolescent multilingual writers* because I believe that adolescent multilingual students engage in writing activities, tasks, or assignments one way or another. I like to highlight their writing practices and see them as writers, although, many of them may neither perceive their everyday, especially out-of-school, writing as writing nor think of themselves as writers (Yi, Kao, & Kang, 2017).

The Aim of the Book

I envision three major goals of the book. First, this book aims to reconceptualize adolescent multilingual writing by (a) exploring in-school and out-of-school writing as well as the connections between the two in a comprehensive manner, (b) proposing a *symbiotic* model of understanding mutually beneficial relationships (interrelated and interdependent) between in-school and out-of-school literate lives, and (c) challenging the deficit perspectives of adolescent multilingual students and their language and literacy practices, as well as promoting asset-based perspectives. I seek to underscore students' strengths rather than weaknesses through a better understanding of the rich, dynamic, and complex writing practices of young people.

Second, this book aims to promote and develop adolescent multilingual writing as an emerging area of inquiry given the lack of attention to and potential importance of adolescent multilingual writing. I hope that adolescent multilingual writing will be a more interdisciplinary inquiry, being influenced from other fields of inquiry, such as composition studies, applied linguistics, second language acquisition, bilingual education, and literacy studies. At the same time, this book strives to widen the perspectives of *adolescent writing and literacy* by considering a much wider range of texts, contexts, skills, knowledge, and experiences of adolescent writers from various linguistic backgrounds. Although my discussions and arguments in this book are focused on adolescent multilingual writers, their implications for research and pedagogy can offer valuable insights into adolescent writing and literacy.

Third, this book aims to be a leading resource in researching issues of adolescent multilingual writers and their writing. It aims to provide researchers and graduate students with a principled overview and synthesis of adolescent multilingual writing research that is significant yet underexplored in applied linguistics, TESOL, and literacy studies. Thus, they will have a better sense of what we know and need to know about adolescent multilingual writing. Furthermore, although this book does not necessarily focus on discussing writing pedagogy or instructional implications, the review and synthesis of literature and my discussions in this book will shed light on ways in which teachers create classroom environments where adolescent multilinguals have access to and engage with a greater variety of textual resources, activities, and experiences.

To this end, this book examines the nature of adolescent multilingual writing from the perspectives of sociocultural theory and literacy as a social practice. This text distinguishes itself from existing texts that typically examine only one aspect of adolescent multilingual writing, such as either in-school, academic writing or informal, out-of-school writing. In addition, unlike much of the literature that highlights how to integrate out-of-school writing into classroom practices, this book attempts to underscore the importance of exploring the relationship between in-school and out-of-school writing in a symbiotic manner.

The primary audience of this book includes professionals and scholars of L2/multilingual literacy education, such as graduate students, in TESOL, applied linguistics, and related fields (e.g., literacy education), as well as scholars and teacher educators who teach and conduct research on L2 writing and literacy in ESL and EFL contexts. Graduate students and scholars with relatively little knowledge about adolescent L2/multilingual writing will obtain a good sense of the issues in adolescent

L2/multilingual writing research offered in this text. The book also provides graduate students and scholars with extensive knowledge of adolescent L2/multilingual writing research with more expanded and critical
insights and perspectives of understanding and exploring adolescent
L2/multilingual writing, writers, and writing pedagogy. In addition,
practitioners will learn more about theoretical and research aspects
of adolescent multilingual writing, and thus, they can explore ways in
which they enact praxis in L2/multilingual literacy instruction.

Organization of the Book

This book is composed of six chapters. The next chapter (Chapter 2)
provides readers with a theoretical foundation to better understand
adolescent multilingual writing research by reviewing and explaining
three of the most dominant perspectives on writing, which are cognitive, sociocultural, and critical perspectives. Instead of treating each
perspective as autonomous, this chapter also addresses the intersections between perspectives.

Chapter 3 focuses on discussing issues of out-of-school, voluntary
writing practices. It is intended to illuminate the rich, diverse, and
meaningful writing practices in which many adolescent multilingual writers engage beyond the classroom. It discusses the value and
characteristics of out-of-school writing (e.g., self-initiated, voluntary,
intentional, interest-driven, peer-driven, multilingual) and illustrates
ways in which adolescent multilingual students write, communicate,
learn, and represent themselves through out-of-school writing across
online, home, community, and workplace contexts.

Shifting the attention from out-of-school writing, the following
chapter (Chapter 4) focuses more on the issues of school-sponsored,
academic writing practices in order to better understand academic
writing experiences and expectations in comparison with out-of-
school writing that is discussed in the previous chapter (Chapter 3).
The chapter begins by defining key terms, *academic language*, *literacy*,
and *writing* and then synthesizes major findings from adolescent multilingual writing research conducted in English-medium classroom
contexts. Major topics discussed in this chapter include (a) types of
writing activities; (b) content area writing; (c) writing processes, strategies, and products; (d) factors influencing academic writing development; and (e) identity and technology.

Drawing upon the discussions about out-of-school and academic
writing in Chapters 3 and 4, Chapter 5 looks into the *connections* between
in-school and out-of-school literate lives. It focuses on discussing how

the connections between the two have been conceptualized in the literature, from earlier conversations to more recent and critical ones. In addition, this chapter proposes an expanded perspective of the connections, or what I term a *symbiotic approach*, which emphasizes exploring and cultivating bi-directional relationships between the two.

This book ends with a brief concluding chapter that summarizes the major arguments and research insight offered in all the previous chapters. It discusses the contributions of the book to the fields of L2 writing and literacy studies, focusing on how this book expands the continuum of literacy research. After discussing its contributions, this chapter concludes with a discussion of future directions in terms of theoretical, methodological, and pedagogical implications for adolescent (multilingual) literacy research and pedagogy.

Notes

1. Although I use the terms "in-school" and "out-of-school" in this book, I acknowledge the false dichotomy of in-school and out-of-school writing and further discuss the blurred boundaries or continuity among adolescents' literacy practices across multiple contexts in Chapter 3. Yet, using terms like in-school and out-of-school can help me explore a symbiotic relationship between in-school and out-of-school writing. In this book, in-school writing refers to school-sponsored, official, and academic writing, whereas out-of-school writing refers to more self-initiated, voluntary, non-academic informal writing. For instance, students' homework for school has typically taken place in an out-of-school physical setting, but is considered an academic activity.
2. Although the latest NAEP writing assessment was conducted in 2017, the report of complete analysis of the data has not been released as of December, 2020.

References

Allard, E. C. (2016). Latecomers: The sources and impacts of late arrival among immigrant students. *Anthropology & Education Quarterly*, *47*(4), 366–384. https://doi.org/10.1111/aeq.12166

Applebee, A. N., & Langer, J. A. (2011). A snapshot of writing instruction in middle school and high schools. *English Journal*, *100*(6), 14–27.

Bialik, K., Scheller, A., & Walker, K. (2018, October 25). *6 facts about English language learners in U.S. public schools*. Pew Research Center. https://www.pewresearch.org/fact-tank/2018/10/25/6-facts-about-english-language-learners-in-u-s-public-schools/

Black, R. W. (2008). *Adolescent and online fan fiction*. New York: Peter Lang.

Bunch, G. (2006). "Academic English" in the 7th grade: Broadening the lens, expanding access. *Journal of English for Academic Purposes*, *5*(4), 284–301. https://doi.org/10.1016/j.jeap.2006.08.007

16   *Adolescent Multilingual Writing*

Christenbury, L., Bomber, R., & Smagorinsky, P. (2010). *Handbook of adolescent literacy research*. New York: The Guilford Press.

Clark, C. T., Blackburn, M. V., & Newell, G. E. (2010). From chasm to conversation: Bridging divides in research on adolescent literacies. *Reading Research Quarterly*, *45*(1), 116–127. https://doi.org/10.1598/RRQ.45.1.6

Clark-Gareca, B., Short, D., Lukes, M., & Sharp-Ross, M. (2020). Long-term English learner: Current research, policy, and practice. *TESOL Journal*, *11*(1), 1–15. https://onlinelibrary.wiley.com/doi/full/10.1002/tesj.452

Cox, M., Jordan, J., Ortmeier-Hooper, C., & Schwartz, G. (Eds.). (2013). *Reinventing identities in second language writing*. Urbana, IL: National Council of Teachers of English.

Cumming, A. (Ed.). (2012). *Adolescent literacies in a multicultural context*. New York: Routledge. https://doi.org/10.4324/9780203120033

Daniel, S. M. (2018). Resettled refugee youth leveraging their out-of-school literacy practices to accomplish schoolwork. *Mind, Culture, and Activity*, *25*(3), 263–277. https://doi.org/10.1080/10749039.2018.1481092

de Oliveira, L. C., & Silva, T. (Eds). (2013). *L2 writing in secondary classrooms: Student experiences, academic issues, and teacher education*. New York: Routledge. https://doi.org/10.4324/9780203082669

Enright, K. A. (2010). Academic literacies and adolescent learners: English for subject-matter secondary classroom. *TESOL Quarterly*, *44*(4), 804–810. https://doi: 10.5054/tq.2010.237336

Enright, K. A., & Gilliland, B. (2011). Multilingual writing in an age of accountability: From policy to practice in U.S. high school classrooms. *Journal of Second Language Writing*, *20*, 182–195. https://doi.org/10.1016/j.jslw.2011.05.006

Enright, K. A., & Wong, J. W. (2018). Relocalizing standards in English language arts: Consequences on functions of literacy. *Critical Inquiry in Language Studies*, *15*(2), 85–114. https://doi.org/10.1080/15427587.2017.1338957

Faggella-Luby, M. N., Ware, S. M., & Capozzoli, A. (2009). Adolescent literacy—Reviewing adolescent literacy reports: Key components and critical questions. *Journal of Literacy Research*, *41*, 453–475. https://doi.org/10.108 0%2F10862960903340199

Faltis, C. J., & Valdés, G. (2010). Educating immigrant students, refugees, and English language learners: A no border perspective. *Yearbook of the National Society for the Study of Education*, *109*(2), 285–296.

Fránquiz, M. E., & Salinas, C. S. (2011). Newcomers developing English literacy through historical thinking and digitized primary sources. *Journal of Second Language Writing*, *20*(3), 196–210. https://doi.org/10.1016/j.jslw.2011.05.004

Goodwin, A. P., & Jiménez, R. T. (2019). From the editors. *Reading Research Quarterly*, *54*(3), 277–278.

Graham, S., Early, J., & Wilcox, K. (2014). Adolescent writing and writing instruction: Introduction to the special issue. *Reading & Writing*, *27*(6), 969–972.

Graham, S., & Perin, D. (2007). What we know, what we still need to know: Teaching adolescents to write. *Scientific Studies of Reading*, *11*(4), 313–335. https://doi.org/10.1080/10888430701530664

Haneda, M., & Monobe, G. (2009). Bilingual and biliteracy practices: Japanese adolescents living in the United States. *Journal of Asian Pacific Communication*, *19*(1), 7–29. https://doi.org/10.1075/japc.19.1.02han

Harklau, L., & Pinnow, R. (2008). Adolescent second-language writing. In L. Christenbury, R. Bomer, & P. Smagorinsky (Eds.), *Handbook of adolescent literacy research* (pp. 126–139). New York: The Guilford Press.

Harushimana, I. (2011). Multilated dreams: African-born refugees in US secondary schools. *Journal of Peace and Justice Studies*, *21*(2), 23–41. https://doi.org/10.5840/peacejustice20112122

Hughes, J. M. & Morrison, L. (2014). The impact of social networking and a multiliteracies pedagogy on English language learners' writer identities. *Writing & Pedagogy*, *6*(3), 607–631. http://doi.org/10.1558/wap.v6i3.607

Jiménez, R. T., Smith, P. H., & Teague, B. L. (2009). Transnational and community literacies for teachers. *Journal of Adolescent &Adult Literacy*, *53*(1), 16–26. https://doi.org/10.1598/JAAL.53.1.2

Jwa, S. (2012). Modeling L2 writer voice: Discoursal positioning in fanfiction writing. *Computers and Composition*, *29*(4), 323–340. https://doi.org/10.1016/j.compcom.2012.10.001

Karam, F. J. (2018). Language and identity construction: The case of a refugee digital bricoleur. *Journal of Adolescent & Adult Literacy*, *61*(5), 511–521. https://doi.org/10.1002/jaal.719

Kibler, A., & Valdés, G. (2016). Conceptualizing language learners: Socioinstitutional mechanisms and their consequences. *The Modern Language Journal*, *100*(S1), 96–116. https://doi.org/10.1111/modl.12310

Kiuhara, S. A., Graham, S., & Hawken, L. S. (2009). Teaching writing to high school students: A national survey. *Journal of Educational Psychology*, *101*, 136–160. https://doi.org/10.1007/s11145-013-9495-7

Kohls, R. (2018). Understanding L2 writers "at risk": A sociocultural perspective. In James P. Lantolf, M. E. Poehner, & M. Swain (Eds.), *The Routledge handbook of sociocultural theory and second language development* (pp. 343–356). New York: Routledge.

Lam, W. S. E. (2004). Second language socialization in a bilingual chat room: Global and local considerations. *Language, Learning and Teaching*, *8*(3), 44–65. http://dx.doi.org/10125/43994

Lam, W. S. E., & Warriner, D. S. (2012). Transnationalism and literacy: Investigating the mobility of people, languages, texts, and practices in contexts of migration. *Reading Research Quarterly*, *47*(2), 191–215. https://doi.org/10.1002/RRQ.016

Leki, I., Cumming, A., & Silva, T. (2008). *A synthesis of research on second language writing in English*. New York: Routledge.

Lerner, R. M., & Steinberg, L. (2009). *The scientific study of adolescent development: Historical and contemporary perspectives*. In R. M. Lerner & L. Steinberg (Eds.), *Handbook of adolescent psychology: Individual bases of adolescent development* (pp. 3–14). John Wiley & Sons Inc. https://doi.org/10.1002/9780470479193.adlpsy001002

Lesko, N. (2012). *Act your age! A cultural construction of adolescence* (2nd ed). New York: Routledge.

Li, G. (2012). Literacy engagement through online and offline communities outside school: English language learners' development as readers and writers. *Theory Into Practice*, 51(4), 312–318. https://doi.org/10.1080/00405841.2012. 726061

Louie, V. (2006). Growing up ethnic in transnational worlds: Identities among second-generation Chinese and Dominicans. *Identities: Global Studies in Culture and Power*, *13*(3), 363–394. https://doi.org/10.1080/10702890600838118

Martin, M. & Suárez-Orozco, C. (2018). What is take: Promising practices for immigrant origin adolescent newcomers. *Theory into Practice*, *57*(2), 82–90. https://doi.org/10.1080/00405841.2018.1425816

Matsuda, P. K. (2003). Second language writing in the twentieth century: A situated historical perspective. In B. Kroll (Ed.), *Exploring the dynamics of second language writing* (pp. 15–34). New York: Cambridge University Press.

McBrien, J. L. (2005). Educational needs and barriers for refugee students in the United States: A review of the literature. *Review of Educational Research*, *75*(3), 329–364. https://doi.org/10.3102%2F00346543075003329

McCarthey, S. J. (1997). Connecting home and school literacy practices in classrooms with diverse populations. *Journal of Literacy Research*, *29*, 145–182. https://doi.org/10.1080%2F10862969709547955

McGinnis, T., Goodstein-Stolzenbrg, A., & Saliani, E. C. (2007). "Indnpride": Online spaces of transnational youth as sites of creative and sophisticated literacy and identity work. *Linguistics and Education*, *18*, 283–304. https:// doi.org/10.1016/j.linged.2007.07.006

Mo, Y., Kopke, R. A., Hawkins, L. K., Troia, G. A., & Olinghouse, N. G. (2014). The neglected "R" in the time of the Common Core. *The Reading Teacher*, *67*, 445–453. https://doi.org/10.1002/trtr.1227

National Center for Education Statistics (2012). *The Nation's Report Card: Writing 2011* (NCES 2012–470). Institute of Education Sciences, U.S. Department of Education, Washington, DC.

National Commission on Writing in America's Schools and Colleges (2003). *The Neglected "R": The Need for a Writing Revolution*. New York: The College Board.

Olsen, L. (2010). *Reparable harm: Fulfilling the unkept promise of educational opportunity for long term English learners*. Long Beach, CA: Californians Together.

Olson, C. B., Scarcella, R. C., & Matuchniak, T. (2015). *Helping English learners to write: Meeting common core standards, grades 6–12*. New York and London: Teachers College Press.

Ortmeier-Hooper, C. (2013). "She doesn't know who I am": The case of a refugee L2 writer in a high school English language arts classroom. In L. de Oliveira & T. Silva (Eds.), *L2 writing in secondary classrooms: Student experiences, academic issues* (pp. 9–26). New York: Routledge.

Ortmeier-Hooper, C., & Enright, K. A. (2011). Mapping new territory: Toward an understanding of adolescent L2 writers and writing in US contexts.

Journal of Second Language Writing, 20, 167–181. https://doi.org/10.1016/j.jslw.2011.05.002

Orellana, M. F., & Reynolds, J. (2008). Cultural modeling: Leveraging bilingual skills for school paraphrasing tasks. *Reading Research Quarterly, 43*(1), 48–65. https://doi.org/10.1598/RRQ.43.1.4

Perin, D, & de la Paz, S., Piantedosi, K. W., & Peercy, M. M. (2017). The writing of language minority students: A literature review on its relation to oral proficiency. *Reading & Writing Quarterly, 33*(5), 465–483. https://doi.org/10.1080/10573569.2016.1247399

Perkins, D. (2009). *Making learning whole: How seven principles of teaching can transform education.* San Francisco, CA: Jossey-Bass.

Popadiuk, N. (2010). Asian international student transition to high school in Canada. *The Qualitative Report, 15*(6), 1523–1548.

Rahimi, M., Halse, C., & Blackmore, J. (2017). Transnational secondary schooling and im/mobile international students. *Australian Educational Researcher, 44*(6), 1–23. https://doi.org/10.1007/s13384-017-0235-x

Rance-Roney, J. (2010). Jump-starting language and schema for English-language learners: Teacher-composed digital jumpstarts for academic reading. *Journal of Adolescent & Adult Literacy, 53*(5). 386–395. https://doi.org/10.1598/JAAL.53.5.4

Roberge, M., Losey, K. M., & Wald M. (Eds.). (2015). *Teaching U.S.-educated multilingual writers: Pedagogical practices from and for the classroom.* Ann Arbor, MI: University of Michigan Press.

Sánchez, P., & Kasum, G. S. (2012). Connecting transnationalism to the classroom and to theories of immigrant student adaptation. *Berkeley Review of Education, 3*(1), 71–93.

Sarigianides, S. T., Lewis, M., & Petrone, R. (2015). How re-thinking adolescence helps re-imagine the teaching of English. *English Journal, 104*(3), 13–18.

Sauer, L., & Ellis, R. (2019). The social lives of adolescent study abroad learners and their L2 development. *Modern Language Journal, 103*(4), 739–762. https://doi.org/10.1111/modl.12589

Scully, J. E. (2016). Going to school in the United States: Voices of adolescent newcomer. *TESOL Journal, 7*(3), 591–620. https://doi.org/10.1002/tesj.226

Sessions, L., Kang, M., & Womack, S. (2016). The neglected "R": Improving writing instruction through iPad apps. *TechTrends, 60*(3), 218–225. https://doi.org/10.1007/s11528-016-0041-8

Shapiro, S., Farrelly, R., & Curry, M. J. (Eds.). (2018). *Educating refugee-background students: Critical issues and dynamic contexts.* Bristol: Multilingual Matters.

Skerrett, A. (2012). Languages and literacies in translocation: Experiences and perspectives of a transnational youth. *Journal of Literacy Research, 44*(4), 364–395. https://doi.org/10.1177%2F1086296X12459511

Souryasack, R., & Lee, J. S. (2007). Drawing on students' experiences, cultures and languages to develop English language writing: Perspectives from three Lao heritage middle school students. *Heritage Language Journal, 5*(1), 79–97.

Stewart, M. A. (2015). "My journey of hope and peace": Learning from adolescent refugees' lived experiences. *Journal of Adolescent & Adult Literacy, 59* (2), 149–159. https://doi.org/10.1002/jaal.445

Sustarsic, M. (2020). The impact of intercultural exchange on secondary school exchange students and their host families. *Journal of International Students, 10*(4), 912–933. https://doi.org/10.32674/jis.v10i4.1042

Tate, T., Warschauer, M., & Kim, Y. S. G. (2019). Learning to compose digitally: The effect of prior computer use and keyboard activity on NAEP writing. *Reading and Writing*, 32, 1–24. https://doi.org/10.1007/s11145-019-09940-z

Taylor, S.K., & Cummins, J. (2011). Second language writing practices, identity, and the academic achievement of children from marginalized social groups: A comprehensive view. *Writing & Pedagogy, 3*(2), 181–188. https://doi.org/10.1558/wap.v3i2.181

Valdés, G. (1999). Incipient bilingualism and the development of English language writing abilities in the secondary school. In C. J. Faltis & P. Wolfe (Eds.), *So much to say: Adolescents, bilingualism, and ESL in the secondary school* (pp. 138–175). New York: Teachers College Press.

Vanek, J., King, K., & Bigelow, M. (2018). Social presence and identity: Facebook in an English language classroom. *Journal of Language, Identity & Education, 17*(4), 236–254. https://doi.org/10.1080/15348458.2018.1442223

Vertovec, S. (2004). Migrant transnationalism and modes of transformation. *International Migration Review, 38*(3), 970–1001. https://doi.org/10.1111/j.1747-7379.2004.tb00226.x

Vollmer, G. (2002). Sociocultural perspectives on second language writing. *ERIC Clearing House on Languages and Linguistics: News Bulletin, 25*(2), 1–3.

Wiltse, L. (2015). Not just 'sunny days': Aboriginal students connect out-of-school literacy resources with school literacy practices. *Literacy, 49*(2), 60–68. https://doi.org/10.1111/lit.12036

Yi, Y. (2009). Adolescent literacy and identity construction among 1.5 generation students: From a transnational perspective. *Journal of Asian Pacific Communication, 19*(1), 100–129. https://doi.org/10.1075/japc.19.1.06yi

Yi, Y. (2010). Identity matters: Theories that help explore adolescent multilingual writers and their identities. In M. Cox, J. Jordan, C. Ortmeier-Hooper, & G. Schwartz (Eds.), *Reinventing identities in second language* (pp. 303–324). Urbana Champaign, IL: National Council of Teachers of English.

Yi, Y., Kao, C., & Kang, J. (2017). Digital multimodal composing practices of adolescent English language learners in an after-school program. In S. Rilling & M. Dantas-Whitney, (Eds.), *TESOL voices: Insider accounts of classroom life* (pp. 49–55). Alexandria, VA: TESOL Press.

Yi, Y., Kao, C., & Kang, J. (2018). Middle school writing in L2. In J. I. Liontas (Ed.), *The TESOL encyclopedia of English language teaching*. Hoboken, NJ: Wiley. https://doi.org/10.1002/9781118784235.eelt0514

2 Conceptual Landscape
Perspectives on Writing

Introduction

In Chapter 1, I introduced some key issues in adolescent multilingual writing research and pedagogy, including tensions and disconnections between in-school and out-of-school writing practices that many adolescent multilingual students experience. This chapter briefly engages a conceptual discussion of three of the most dominant perspectives on writing, such as cognitive, sociocultural, and critical perspectives, which will help readers better understand adolescent multilingual writing research and pedagogy. Conceptual or theoretical frameworks are crucial in exploring issues in writing because they provide researchers and practitioners with the lenses through which they make sense of writing. Researchers use frameworks to conceptualize L2 writing research, analyze and interpret their data, and report on their findings. Educators use them to (re)design, implement, evaluate, and align curriculum, instruction, and assessment for L2/multilingual learners of writing.

During the past centuries, writing has been viewed through different perspectives. Each perspective has impacted how writing is conceptualized, investigated, and taught; additionally, collectively, these multiple views of writing have provided researchers with "a rich context for thinking about writing" (Graham, 2018, p. 217). While there are some variations in terms of names and focuses to describe each perspective, this chapter uses the three terms, *cognitive, sociocultural,* and *critical* as umbrella terms. Instead of treating each perspective as "autonomous or self-contained" (Ferris & Hedgcock, 2014, p. 63) or completely mutually exclusive, this chapter also addresses the intersections between perspectives. I also remind readers that despite the exploratory or explanatory power of conceptual or theoretical frameworks, no single framework or theory can fully account for the multiplicity and complexity of the nature of L2 writing (Cumming, 2016).

Cognitive Perspective on Writing

One of the most dominant frameworks employed to examine writing is a cognitive perspective or cognitive models of writing. Early writing research from this perspective was conducted by cognitive psychologists examining writing processes by native English speakers (e.g., Hayes & Flower, 1980). While cognitive psychologists view writing as psychological problem-solving, they have examined the internal, cognitive processes involved in writing. From this perspective, writing processes are defined "as those that happen internally within the writer" (Hayes & Olinghouse, 2015, p. 491). Research on the cognitive processes of writing flourished in the 1980s, and this perspective became one of the major approaches to conceptualizing writing in L1 and L2 research for the past 40 years (Graham, 2018; MacArthur, Graham, & Fitzgerald, 2016). Here I explain the two most significant cognitive models of writing, such as Hayes' (2012) and Bereiter and Scardamalia's (1987) models.

In the 1980s, one of the earliest cognitive writing models was proposed in the article, *A Cognitive Process Theory of Writing* by Flower and Hayes (1981). They presented a framework as a working hypothesis to explain the cognitive processes of writers. They attempted to depart from a traditional product-based view of writing process which was seen as "a linear series of stages, separated in time, and characterized by the gradual development of the written product" (pp. 366–367). Instead of seeing writing as a linear process or a stage of plan-write-edit, their process-based models include "a hierarchical structure" (p. 367) and reflect the recursive nature of the process in writing.

Approximately 30 years later, Hayes (2012) presented the revised model of writing based on his earlier models (e.g., Flower & Hayes, 1981; Hayes, 1996). The revised model of writing, which is considered the most comprehensive cognitive model, consists of three levels: (a) control, (b) process, and (c) resource levels (from top to bottom). *The Resource Level* (the bottom level) represents and explains general cognitive resources that individual writers tend to draw upon as they write. There are four resources at the resource level: reading, working memory, long-term memory, and attention (an ability to maintain focus on a task).

The Process Level (the middle level) consists of two parts: the internal "writing processes" (proposer, translator, evaluator, and transcriber) and the "task environment" where these processes operate (Hayes & Olinghouse, 2015, p. 483). The proposer suggests ideas for what should be included in the text and passes the ideas in a nonverbal form on to the translator. Then the translator takes ideas from the proposer and translates these non-verbal ideas into a verbal form of expression by turning ideas into words. The transcriber turns the grammatical strings produced by the translator into written text, that is putting the grammatical strings onto paper. The evaluator finally examines the output of any of the other processes and checks accuracy. In addition to the writing processes, the "task environment" is part of the Process Level. For this model, socially determined factors are all represented in the task environment. It includes the social and physical factors influencing the writing processes. The social task environment includes input from collaborators and critics. The physical task environment includes task materials (e.g., writing worksheet or dictionary), transcribing technology (e.g., handwriting, keyboarding, texting), and the text written so far.

Finally, the *Control Level* (located at the top level) includes "factors that shape and direct the writing activity" (Hayes & Olinghouse, 2015, p. 482), such as (a) "motivation" that is vital to get people to engage in and sustain writing; (b) "goal setting" for the text (e.g., different goals for planning, writing, and revising); (c) "current plan" (goals and sub-goals for creating a current text); and (d) "writing schemas" that represent the writers' knowledge about genre, structures, formats, and writing strategies.

Overall, this revised, latest model of writing includes some substantial changes from the initial model, especially with respect to "what should be included in such models (e.g., adding transcription and motivation) and how it should be represented (e.g., re-representing planning and revision)" (Hayes, 2012, p. 387). One important note here is that in this model Hayes (2012) intended to describe writing processes by adult writers; however, he and his colleagues further attempted to apply cognitive writing models for different populations later. For instance, while addressing K-12 student writers, Hayes and Olinghouse (2015) tried to apply the model to inform the design of the Common Core State Standards in the US context; furthermore Hayes and Berninger (2014), while considering students with disabilities, also applied the same model to predict the effects of disabilities on specific cognitive writing processes and to provide the appropriate support for the affected processes that were involved in writing. As one of the most comprehensive cognitive models of writing, it seems to have a more explanatory power to account for the writing processes; however, Hayes and Olinghouse (2015) noted that this model should be "viewed as work in progress rather than as a finished product" (p. 482).

Another significant cognitive model of writing is the Bereiter and Scardamalia's (1987) model of writing process. While seeing writing as a process of discovery, Bereiter and Scardamalia characterized the difference between novice and expert writers as a contrast between a "knowledge-telling" model of writing and a "knowledge-trans-forming" model of writing, which became one of the significant contributions of cognitive models of writing to writing research and pedagogy. According to the knowledge-telling model, novice writers tend to employ a knowledge-telling strategy in which content is generated from long-term memory with topical cues and extracted from the task assignment, as well as writers locate genre identifies, like structural cues drawn from the genre knowledge (Bereiter, Burtis, & Scardamalia, 1988). This is like a process of young children writing what they know about a certain topic as if they simply tell serially.

However, more advanced and expert writers tend to use a knowl-edge-transforming strategy, that is, writing beyond the telling stage. They tend to analyze, reflect, adjust, update, and revise their knowl-edge and ideas as they write to conform to "their goals [of composi-tion], audience concerns, knowledge of text and language conventions, and evaluations of text produced thus far" (Cumming, 2016, p. 70). They tend to engage in more interactive solution of content problems (e.g., figuring out what the critical issue relating to the topic is) and rhe-torical problems (e.g., deciding which point would be most convincing to strengthen an argument). They tend to "develop a more elaborate representation of their rhetorical goals and use this to develop a fuller representation of the text in rhetorical problem space" (Galbraith, 2009, p. 6). Consequently, they tend to develop more detailed plans before writing as well as revise their plans and initial drafts of texts more substantively during writing. As a result, their texts are likely more tailored to the needs of readers.

Overall, from the cognitive perspective, writing is seen as a cogni-tive process that takes place within individuals. Research from this perspective tends to focus on identifying and elucidating the cognitive processes and strategies involved in writing. In addition, it examines how the cognitive processes (e.g., planning, translating, and review-ing) interact during writing, which reflects the recursive nature of writing (see Alamargot and Chanquoy, 2012, and Becker, 2006, for comprehensive reviews of cognitive writing models).

Although such a cognitive perspective has greatly influenced and contributed to writing research, it was developed solely based on cog-nitive assumptions. By conceptualizing writing as a set of decontextu-alized, discrete skills and strategies that students need to master, the cognitive perspective or theory overlooks the sociocultural, political, and historical contexts of writing (Prior, 2006) and fails to address social dimensions of writing (Nystrand, 1989). In addition, a cognitive perspective or approach alone is not sufficient to explain the nature of writing development and to understand the needs of linguistically and culturally diverse writers. Thus, socially-oriented perspectives and theories seem to represent the dominant paradigm for writing research in more recent years (Prior, 2006).

Sociocultural Perspective on Writing

The "social turn" in writing studies has produced critical conversations about the (re)conceptualization of writing, and a growing body of empirical research has examined social aspects of writing (Prior, 2006). A sociocultural perspective has been influenced by sociocultural theory and often framed in Vygotskian terms. Differing from the cognitive perspective on writing that frames writing development as the "acquisition of text-level psychological skills or cognitive processes employed by individual writers to compose a written text" (Beach, Newell, & VanDerHeide, 2016, p. 89), a sociocultural perspective views writing as a form of social practice, event, and action (Kostouli, 2009). Pioneers of the sociocultural view, Scribner and Cole (1981), articulated the paradigm shift from psychological to social in understanding literacy and conducting literacy studies as noted in the following oft-cited quote:

> Instead of focusing exclusively on the technology of a writing system and its reputed consequences.... We approach literacy as a set of socially organized practices which make use of a symbol of system and a technology for producing and disseminating it. Literacy is not simply knowing how to read and write a particular script but applying this knowledge for specific purposes in specific contexts of use. The nature of these practices, including, of course, their technical aspects, will determine the kinds of skills ("consequences") associated with literacy.
>
> (Scribner & Cole, 1981, p. 236)

Carmen Luke (2003) later stated that such a shift from a psychological to a social paradigm marks "the last breakthrough" in literacy research (p. 401).

   More specifically, what most distinguishes a sociocultural from a cognitive perspective is that "a sociocultural perspective foregrounds the *social practices* student writers acquire through social and cultural contexts for their writing" (Beach, Newell, & VanDerHeide, 2016, p. 90).

Writing is primarily what people do, as noted "it is an activity, located in the space between thought and text... [It] is essentially social, and it is located in the interaction between people" (Barton & Hamilton, 1998, p.3). This perspective highlights the importance of understanding "the historical, economic, political, and socio-cultural context" in which writing takes place (McKay, 1993, p. 8), and how writing is used and valued in such contexts because it maintains that contexts fundamentally shape the way writing gets done. Since sociocultural theory tends to foreground writers in multiple contexts (Kohls, 2018), this perspective has been extensively used in research that explores writers and writing across various contexts (e.g., home, school, online, community). Readers will find that many out-of-school writing studies discussed in the next chapter (Chapter 3) have been situated within a sociocultural perspective on writing.

Furthermore, from this perspective, writing is *situated* in and across contexts and is a *mediated process* through which writers employ various resources (e.g., multiple languages, non-linguistic resources, technologies) that influence the nature of writing (Bazerman, 2016; Cook-Gumperz, 1986; McKay, 1993; Prior, 2006; Street, 1984). Writing development means the learning of the practices, values, norms, and genres of the community where writing is used, and thus, proficient multilingual writers are those who can "act effectively in new cultural settings" (Hyland, 2002, p. 60).

Within the sociocultural perspective, a noteworthy notion is multiliteracies that stresses the "plurality" of literacy conceptualized by the New London Group (NLG) (1996). This concept of multiliteracies is especially compelling when we investigate and discuss the writing practices and development of students from diverse linguistic and cultural backgrounds, like multilingual writers who are likely to navigate across various writing contexts. Globally and locally, more and more people engage in "multiple sets of literacy practices" in their daily lives (Kern, 2000, p. 75). Those who experience multiple languages and literacies tend to take "multiple paths" to the learning of different languages and are equipped with different degrees of expertise in these languages and literacies (Martin-Jones & Jones, 2000, p. 7). In addition, the concept of multiliteracies is an essential notion in our digitally-mediated society. The development of emerging digital technologies has produced new literacy contexts and varying types of literacy activities (e.g., emailing, instant-messaging, web-surfing). According to McKay (1995), "different contexts demand a different type of literacy expertise" (p. 421). For instance, instant messages may differ from e-mail messages or print-based letters. Thus, the concept of multiliteracies is important to understand current and future individuals who experience multiple languages and writing across multiple literacy contexts. Furthermore, a thorough understanding of multiple sets of literacies can help teachers enable their students to make a smooth transition to meet various demands for different uses and purposes of writing in their day-to-day lives.

Barton and Hamilton (1998) aptly summarize the sociocultural view of literacy in the form of six propositions, presenting the theory of literacy as social practice. Although they address literacy in a comprehensive sense, these propositions can capture the essence of a sociocultural perspective on writing:

- Literacy is best understood as a set of social practices; these can be inferred from events which are mediated by written texts.
- There are different literacies associated with different domains of life.
- Literacy practices are patterned by social institutions and power relationships, and some literacies are more dominant, visible, and influential than others.
- Literacy practices are purposeful and embedded in broader social goals and cultural practices.
- Literacy is historically situated.
- Literacy practices change and new ones are frequently acquired through processes of informal learning and sense making (p. 8).

Finally, it is important to note that a sociocultural perspective does not ignore the importance of *cognition* and *cognitive processes* nor the development of writing/literacy *skills*. In other words, the perspective of writing as social practice "is not to deny the role of cognitive and linguistic processes" (Newell et al., 2011, p. 288). As noted, scholars holding a sociocultural view believe that writing and even cognition are situated within broader institutional, sociocultural, political, and historical contexts where writing takes place (Prior, 2006). That is, this perspective still considers cognition but focuses more on social dimensions. Overall, a sociocultural perspective on writing has provided researchers and educators with a robust theoretical and conceptual lens through which they better understand adolescent multilingual writers across various contexts in which writing takes place (Kohls, 2018).

Yet, a group of scholars maintain that the sociocultural perspective has generally ignored the "cognitive and motivational resources" writers use while writing (Graham, 2018, p. 218). Thus, they have adopted a *socio-cognitive* perspective while taking the intersectional perspective between cognitive and sociocultural perspectives. A socio-cognitive perspective conceptualizes writing while incorporating both cognitive and social perspectives, given that one perspective has minimally considered another. For instance, Deane (2018) contends that "writing is both an individual performance and a social practice" (p. 280), and that sociocultural factors often interact with cognitive ones. For instance, sociocultural contexts influence how writers choose their cognitive strategies for writing. When students write a school essay for their grades, they may ask for feedback on their drafts, produce multiple drafts, and engage in several revisions. Yet, when they engage in writing a grocery shopping list, they employ different writing strategies (e.g., using images or abbreviations). Drawing upon socio-cognitive theory, L2 writing research has focused on examining ways in which individual writers learn to engage in socially and historically situated activities, such as disciplinary writing. For instance, Wilcox (2011) examined both contextual and individual cognitive factors that came into play in secondary ELs' development of disciplinary writing. As such, a socio-cognitive perspective on writing addresses the intersections between cognitive and sociocultural perspectives.

Critical Perspective on Writing

Critical approaches to literacy begun with concerns about social inequalities, power relationships, identity, and human agency (Mills, 2016). One of the most defining characteristics of critical theory and perspective is that it centers on *power relationships*. Perry (2012) maintains that critical theory adds power relationships to a sociocultural perspective. In other words, a critical perspective on writing and literacy extends a sociocultural perspective by foregrounding power relationships in writing practices. Similarly, critical literacy studies explore and explain "the relationship between language use and power" (Perry, 2012, p. 52). For instance, emails sent to classmates and a professor asking questions about a final exam would look different from one another. A research grant proposal to a funding agency may look different from a student's research proposal for a class project. Here it is evident that writing would change depending on whom you write to because it always entails power dynamics.

From the critical perspective, everything is power-ridden and nothing is neutral. No text is neutral or value-free. Neither is teaching and learning writing and literacy. Literacy is more than the acquisition of a set of cognitive skills, but is understood as "the relationship of learners to the world" (Freire & Macedo, 1998, p. 173). Thus, focusing on power, a critical perspective helps understand how writing and literacy practices are shaped by power relationships and social institutions. For instance, teaching a certain kind of writing can benefit a certain group of students. Argumentative writing is considered one of the most significant genres to teach in school because of standards and high-stakes testing, which, in turn, influences writing instruction that places heavy emphasis on teaching this particular genre over others. Then, students who are more exposed to and familiar with this argumentative genre in their daily lives would benefit more than those who may engage more in narrative or creative writing outside of school. Furthermore, this perspective helps raise our awareness of the importance of individual's agency in adopting, appropriating, or rejecting practices to meet their own needs.

Although there is no agreed or set definition of critical literacy, Lewison, Flint, and Van Sluys (2002) synthesized a wide range of definitions from the literature into four common dimensions, which captures a critical perspective on writing and literacy in a comprehensive manner: "(1) disrupting the commonplace, (2) interrogating multiple viewpoints, (3) focusing on sociopolitical issues, and (4) taking action and promoting social justice" (p. 382).

In order to disrupt the commonplace, teachers and students are encouraged to problematize unchallenged assumptions and interrogate texts by asking questions such as "How people are positioned by this particular text?"; "How does this text solidify or disrupt the status quo?"; and "How texts are used to benefit certain groups of people?" Second, critical literacy encourages educators to examine multiple perspectives, especially contradictory and competing ones concurrently, for instance by asking such questions as "Whose voices are heard and whose are missing?". Third, critical literacy asks people to pay attention to sociopolitical systems where they belong and challenge unequal power relationships by investigating the relationship between language and power. The fourth dimension, "taking action and promotion social justice" is often considered the primary purpose of critical literacy, but the other three dimensions collectively help people take action for social change (Lewison, Flint, & Van Sluys, 2002, pp. 382–384).

These four dimensions demonstrate that critical literacy can take multiple forms, such as critically analyzing various authentic texts that students encounter in school, at home, and in society; writing counter-narratives and counter-arguments; engaging in social change projects; and discussing sociopolitical issues (e.g., discrimination, violence, poverty) in class. Centrally, critical literacy education aims to equip young people with a *perspective* and *language of critique* to critically analyze, question, and challenge dominant social norms, assumptions, and ideology embedded in texts and to rewrite texts in such a way that "their interest, identities, and legitimate aspirations are more fully present and are present more equally" (Lankshear & McLaren, 1993, p. xviii).

Some other scholars have proposed models of critical literacy, such as Freebody and Luke's *Four Resources Model* (Freebody & Luke, 1990; Luke & Freebody, 1999) and Janks' *Synthesis Model of Critical Literacy* (Janks, 2000, 2010). The Four Resources Model (Freebody & Luke, 1990) originally included the four roles of readers as (a) code breaker, (b) text participant, (c) text user, and (d) text analyst. Later they revised their original concept of "roles" to "practices" that readers and writers draw upon for meaning-making (Luke & Freebody, 1999). Four practices include (a) breaking the code of texts (recognizing and using basic features of written text like alphabet knowledge), (b) participating in the meanings of text (comprehending and composing meaningful texts), (c) using texts functionally (using text for particular purposes), and (d) critically analyzing and transforming texts (understanding that texts are not neutral and are constructed for specific purposes) (Luke & Freebody, 1999, pp. 7–8).

Janks' Synthesis Model of Critical Literacy (Janks, 2000, 2010) is one of the most significant models of critical literacy and is quite similar to the four dimensions of critical literacy synthesized by Lewison, Flint, and Van Sluys (2002). Janks synthesized four existing orientations in critical literacy education: domination, access, diversity, and design. Critical theorists foregrounding *domination* see language and discourse as a means of preserving, reproducing, and regulating relations of power. They assert that any text constructed can be de-constructed. It is important for readers to de-construct texts (e.g., through critical discourse analysis) while asking questions; "Why did the author make such choices to construct the text (e.g., choices of genre, specific language, images selected, color, layout)?" and "Whose interests does this text serve?" *Access* is one of the key issues in education. Access to the language of power and the dominant forms (e.g., dominant genres) is especially valuable in helping ELs with academic achievement and social success. Janks argues for the balance between critique and access.

The last two orientations, *diversity* and *design* refer, respectively, to the inclusion of students' diverse ways of reading and writing which are "a central resource for changing consciousness" (Janks, 2000, p. 177) and "the ability to harness the multiplicity of semiotic systems across diverse cultural locations to challenge and change existing Discourses" (p. 177). New Literacy Studies (NLS) and multiliteracies offer some good examples of the implications of diversity and design, respectively. The NLS's perspective of literacy as socially situated practices in any given context encourages researchers to examine multiple ways of reading, writing, thinking, and valuing, including critically reflecting on their own taken-for-granted ways of doing so. Multiliteracies (Cope & Kalantzis, 2000; New London Group, 1996) considers reader, writer, and viewer as "designers" of meaning. When they design (write) texts, they engage in multimodal practices, employing multiple modes for meaning-making, such as images, music, and gestures. While critical literacy with a domination orientation tends to emphasize critical reading (e.g., deconstruction), the design-oriented critical literacy work emphasizes multimodal (re)design using a range of modes and media. Importantly, Janks highlights the interdependence of all the four orientations, with each being important, to achieve social justice.

In the field of applied linguistics, there has also been growing interest in examining the intersection of language/literacy with sociopolitical issues (e.g., race, class, gender, power inequality, social structures) from a critical perspective (Benesch, 1999; Chun, 2016; Kim & Cho, 2017; Kubota, 2018; Lau, Juby-Smith, & Desbiens, 2017; Yoon, Simpson, & Haag, 2010). The majority of studies on critical literacy practices have been conducted in the classroom contexts, with some exceptions (e.g., Kabuto, 2006), and thus relatively little is known about ways in which multilingual students engage in critical literacy practices in out-of-school settings. In fact, Haneda (2006) posited that critical literacy practice and pedagogy could be a way to foster connections among school, home, and community for multilingual students. She further suggested that teachers design classroom environments where students express their ideas freely and discuss sociopolitical issues students often encounter at home while using reading and writing as significant tools for reflection, evaluation, and critique. In such classroom contexts, students could engage in such practices as breaking the code of texts, participating in the meanings of text, using texts for particular purposes, and critically analyzing and transforming texts (Luke & Freebody, 1999). In reality, some teachers express concerns that critical literacy is too difficult for young people; others have experienced a tension between a rigid curriculum focusing on teaching basic reading and writing skills and critical literacy instruction (Eastman, 1998; Perkins, 1998). In addition, particularly for multilingual students, some teachers believe advanced L2 literacy skills are prerequisite to critical literacy practices. All these beliefs of teachers seem to prevent them from incorporating critical literacy practices into classrooms.

Finally, there is a group of scholars who acknowledge the intersections between sociocultural and critical perspectives and straddle sociocultural and critical literacy research. For instance, Brian Street's work is instrumental to the New Literacy Studies which was one of significant movements that took place in a social turn; additionally, he proposed an "ideological model of literacy" (Street, 1984) which addresses literacy in relation to larger social contexts and power relationships. Both sociocultural and critical approaches to writing and literacy emphasize the social (Mills, 2016), and some sociocultural researchers, while drawing from critical theory, have explored writing and literacy practices in relation to power, access to literacies, marginalization, and so forth (Ajayi, 2008; Harman, 2018). Given some intersections between the two perspectives, some scholars like Lewis, Enciso, and Moje (2007) proposed a "critical sociocultural approach" to literacy research in response to a growing criticism that the sociocultural perspective has not overtly addressed "important issues of identity, agency, and power in the production of knowledge that are central to understanding literacy as a social and cultural practice" (p. xi). This critical sociocultural perspective has not been extensively used in L2 literacy research, yet it could be a promising framework for critical discussions and investigations of ways in which multilingual students achieve access and equity in writing and literacy learning (e.g., Teemant, 2015).

Summary of Perspectives on Writing

In this chapter, three major perspectives on writing – cognitive, sociocultural, and critical – were explored to help researchers and practitioners better understand adolescent multilingual writing research. These perspectives have helped advance research and pedagogy in applied linguistics, TESOL, and literacy studies. Despite some intersections among these perspectives, each has distinct characteristics and has uniquely contributed to writing and literacy research. Typically using a quantitative research methodology, writing research from a cognitive perspective tends to focus on examining cognitive processes and strategies involved in writing. Studies from sociocultural and critical perspectives have usually employed a qualitative research methodology and examined writers and writing within social contexts (e.g., home, online, workplaces) and writing practices in relation to identity, agency, and power relationships. Over the past decades, empirical research on writing has increasingly drawn upon sociocultural theories (Prior, 2006), and thus, much of the recent research on adolescent multilingual writing outside of school (Chapter 3) and in school (Chapter 4) has been conceptualized within sociocultural perspectives. Finally, despite of the exploratory and explanatory power of these theoretical and conceptual frameworks, researchers still face challenges of accounting for the complex, dynamic, and multiple nature of multilingual writing in a comprehensive manner (Cumming, 2016).

References

Ajayi, L. (2008). Meaning-making, multimodal representations, and transformative pedagogy: An exploration of meaning constructional practices in an ESL high school classroom. *Journal of Language, Identity, and Education, 7,* 206–229. https://doi.org/ 10.1080/25348450802237822

Alamargot, D. & Chanquoy, L. (2012). Through the models of writing: Ten years after and vision for the future. In V. W. Berninger (Ed.), *Past, present, and future contributions of cognitive writing research to cognitive psychology* (pp. 567–572). New York: Psychology Press. https://doi.org/10.4324/9780203805312

Barton, D., & Hamilton, M. (1998). *Local literacies: Reading and writing in one community.* London: Routledge. https://doi.org/10.4324/9780203125106

Bazerman, C. (2016). What do sociocultural studies of writing tell us about learning to write? In C. MacArthur, S., Graham & J. Fitzgerald (Eds.), *Handbook of writing research* (pp. 11–23). New York: Guilford Press.

Beach, R., Newell, G., & VanDerHeide, J. (2016). A sociocultural perspective on writing development: Toward an agenda for classroom research on students' use of social practices. In C. MacArthur, S., Graham & J. Fitzgerald (Eds.), *Handbook of writing research* (pp. 88–101). New York: Guilford Press.

Becker, A (2006). A review of writing model research based on cognitive processes. In A. Horning & A. Becker (Eds.), *Revision: History, theory, and practice* (pp. 25–49). West Lafayette, IN: Parlor Press.

Benesch, S. (1999). Thinking critically, thinking dialogically. *TESOL Quarterly, 33* (3), 573–580. https://doi.org/10.2307/3587682

Bereiter, C., Burtis, P. J., & Scardamalia, M. (1988). Cognitive operations in constructing main points in written composition. *Journal of Memory and Language, 27*(3), 261–278. https://doi.org/10.1016/0749-596X(88)90054-X

Bereiter, C. & Scardamalia, M. (Eds.) (1987). *The psychology of written composition.* Hillsdale, NJ: Erlbaum. https://doi.org/10.4324/9780203812310

Chun, C. (2016). Critical literacy writing in ESP: Perspectives and approaches. In J. Flowerdew & T. Costley (Eds.), *Discipline-specific writing: Theory into practice* (pp. 181–195). London: Routledge. https://doi.org/10.4324/9781315519012

Cook-Gumperz, J. (Ed.). (1986). *The social construction of literacy.* Cambridge, UK: Cambridge University Press.

34 *Conceptual Landscape*

Cope, B., & Kalantzis, M. (Eds.) (2000). *Multiliteracies: Literacy learning and the design of social futures*. New York: Routledge.

Cumming, A. (2016). Theoretical orientations to L2 writing. In Rosa M. Manchón & P. K. Matsuda (Eds.), *Handbook of second and foreign language writing* (pp. 65–88). Boston, MA: Walter De Gruyter Mouton. https://doi.org/10.1515/9781614511335

Deane, P. (2018). The challenges of writing in school: Conceptualizing writing development within a sociocognitive framework. *Educational Psychologist*, *53*(4), 280–300. https://doi.org/10.1080/00461520.2018.1513844

Eastman, L. (1998). Oral discussion in teaching critical literacy to beginners. In A. Burns & S. Hood (Eds.), *Teachers' voices 3: Teaching critical literacy* (pp. 22–28). Sydney, Australia: National Centre for English Language Teaching and Research, Macquarie University.

Ferris, D. R., & Hedgcock, J. S. (2014). *Teaching L2 composition: Purpose, process, and practice* (3rd ed.). New York: Routledge. https://doi.org/10.4324/9780203813003

Flower, L., & Hayes, J. (1981) A cognitive process theory of writing. *College Composition and Communication*, *32*(4), 365–387.

Freebody, P., & Luke, A. (1990). Literacies programs: Debates and demands in cultural context. *Prospect: An Australian Journal of TESOL*, 5(3), 7–16.

Freire, A. M. A., & Macedo, D. (Eds). (1998). *The Paulo Freire reader*. New York: Continuum.

Galbraith, D. (2009). Writing as discovery. *British Journal of Educational Psychology*, *1*(1), 5–26. https://doi.org/10.1348/978185409X421129

Graham, S. (2018). Introduction to conceptualizing writing. *Educational Psychologist*, *53*(4), 217–219. https://doi.org/10.1080/00461520.2018.1514303

Haneda, M. (2006). Becoming literate in a second language: Connecting home, community, and school literacy practices. *Theory into Practice*, *45*, 337–345. https://doi.org/10.1207/s15430421tip4504_7

Harman, R. (Ed.) (2018). *Bilingual learners and social equity: Critical approaches to systemic functional linguistics*. London, UK: Springer. https://doi.org/10.1007/978-3-319-60953-9

Hayes, J. R. (1996). A new framework for understanding cognition and affect in writing. In C. M. Levy & S. Ransdell (Eds.), *The science of writing: Theories, methods, individual differences, and applications* (pp. 1–27). New York: Routledge. https://doi.org/10.4324/9780203811122

Hayes, J. R. (2012). Modeling and remodeling writing. *Written Communication*, *29*(3), 369–388. https://doi.org/10.1177/0741088312451260

Hayes, J. R., & Berninger, V. (2014). Cognitive processes in writing: A framework. In B. Arfé, J. E. Dockrell & V.W. Berninger (Eds.), *Writing development and instruction in children with hearing loss, dyslexia or oral language problems: Implications for assessment and instruction* (pp. 3–15). New York: Oxford University Press.

Hayes, J. R., & Flower, L. (1980). Identifying the organization of writing processes. In L. W. Gregg & E. R. Steinberg (Eds.), *Cognitive processes in writing: An interdisciplinary approach* (pp. 3–30). Hillsdale, NJ: Lawrence Erlbaum.

Hayes, J. R., & Olinghouse, N.G. (2015). Can cognitive writing models inform the design of the Common Core State Standards? *The Elementary School Journal, 115*(4), 480–497. https://doi.org/10.1086/681909

Hyland, K. (2002). *Teaching and researching writing*. London: Longman.

Janks, H. (2000). Domination, access, diversity and design: A synthesis for critical literacy education. *Educational Review, 52*(2), 175–186. https://doi.org/10.1080/713664035

Janks, H. (2010). *Literacy and power*. New York: Taylor & Francis. https://doi.org/10.4324/9780203869956

Kabuto, B. (2006). *Becoming biliterate: Identity, ideology, and learning to read and write in two languages*. New York: Routledge. https://doi.org/10.4324/9780203846438

Kern, R. (2000). *Literacy and language teaching*. New York: Oxford University Press.

Kim, S., & Cho, H. (2017). Reading outside the box: Exploring critical literacy with Korean preschool children. *Language & Education, 31*(2), 110–129. https://doi.org/10.1080/09500782.2016.1263314

Kohls, R. (2018). Understanding L2 writers "at risk": A sociocultural perspective. In J. P. Lantolf, M. E. Poehner & M. Swain (Eds.), *The Routledge handbook of sociocultural theory and second language development* (pp. 343–356). New York: Routledge. https://doi.org/10.4324/9781315624747

Kostouli, T. (2009). A sociocultural framework: Writing as social practice. In R. Beard, D. Myhill, M. Nystrand & J. Riley (Eds.), *The SAGE handbook of writing development* (pp. 98–116). London: SAGE. http://dx.doi.org/10.4135/9780857021069.n7

Kubota, R. (2018). Critical approaches to second language writing. In J. I. Liontas (Ed.), *The TESOL encyclopedia of English language teaching*. Malden, MA: Wiley-Blackwell. https://doi.org/10.1002/9781118784235.eelt0525

Lankshear, C., & McLaren, P. (Eds.). (1993). *Critical literacy: Politics, praxis, and the postmodern*. Albany, NY: State University of New York Press.

Lau, S. M. C., Juby-Smith, B., & Desbiens, I. (2017). Translanguaging for transgressive praxis: Promoting critical literacy in a multiage bilingual classroom. *Critical Inquiry in Language Studies, 14*(1), 1–29. https://doi.org/10.1080/15427587.2016.1242371

Lewis, C., Enciso, P., & Moje, E. (Eds.) (2007). *Reframing sociocultural research on literacy: Identity, agency, and power*. New York: Routledge. https://doi.org/10.4324/9781003064428

Lewison, M., Flint, A.S., & Van Sluys, K. (2002). Taking on critical literacy: The journey of newcomers and novices. *Language Arts, 79*(5), 382–392.

Luke, A., & Freebody, P. (1999). A map of possible practices: Further notes on the four resources model. *Practically Primary, 4*(2), 5–8.

Luke, C. (2003). Pedagogy, connectivity, multimodality, and interdisciplinarity. *Reading Research Quarterly, 38*(3), 397–403.

MacArthur, C. A., Graham, S., & Fitzgerald, J. (2016). *Handbook of writing research* (2nd ed.). New York: Guilford.

McKay, S. L. (1993). *Agendas for second language literacy.* Cambridge, MA: Cambridge Language Education.

McKay, S. L. (1995). Literacy and literacies. In S. L. McKay & N. Hornberger (Eds.), *Sociolinguistics and language teaching* (pp. 421–445). Cambridge, MA: Cambridge University Press.

Martin-Jones, M., & Jones, K. (2000). (Eds.). *Multilingual literacies: reading and writing in different worlds.* Amsterdam, the Netherlands: John Benjamins.

Mills, K. (2016). *Literacy theories for the digital age: Social, critical, multimodal, spatial, material, and sensory lenses.* Bristol: Multilingual Matters https://doi.org/10.21832/9781783094639

New London Group. (1996). A pedagogy of multiliteracies: Designing social futures. *Harvard Educational Review, 66*(1), 60–92. https://doi.org/10.17763/haer.66.1.17370n67v22j160u

Newell, G. E., Beach, R., Smith, J., & VanDerHeide, J. (2011). Teaching and learning argumentative reading and writing: A review of research. *Reading Research Quarterly, 46*(3), 273–304. https://doi.org/10.1598/RRQ.46.3.4

Nystrand, M. (1989). A social-interactive model of writing. *Written Communication, 6*(1), 66–85. https://doi.org/10.1177/0741088389006001005

Perkins, J. (1998). Developing critical literacy with post-beginner learners. In A. Burns & S. Hood (Eds.), *Teachers' voices 3: Teaching critical literacy* (pp. 29–39). Sydney, Australia: National Centre for English Language Teaching and Research, Macquarie University.

Perry, K. H. (2012). What Is literacy? – A critical overview of sociocultural perspectives. *Journal of Language and Literacy Education, 8*(1), 50–71.

Prior, P. (2006). A sociocultural theory of writing. In C. MacArthur, S. Graham & J. Fitzgerald (Eds.), *Handbook of writing research* (pp. 54–66). New York: Guilford Press.

Scribner, S., & Cole, M. (1981). *The psychology of literacy.* Cambridge, MA: Harvard University Press.

Street, B. (1984). *Literacy in theory and practice.* Cambridge, UK: Cambridge University Press.

Teemant, A. (2015, Fall). Living critical sociocultural theory in classroom practice. *Minnesota TESOL Journal.* http://minnetesoljournal.org/fall-2015/living-critical-sociocultural-theory-in-classroom-practice

Wilcox, K. C. (2011). Writing across the curriculum for secondary school English language learners: A case study. *Writing & Pedagogy, 3* (1), 79–111. https://doi.org/10.1558/wap.v3i1.79

Yoon, B., Simpson, A., & Haag, C. (2010). Assimilation ideology: Critically examining underlying messages in multicultural literature. *Journal of Adolescent & Adult Literacy, 54*(2), 109–118. https://doi.org/10.1598/JAAL.54.2.3

3 Adolescent Multilingual Writing Outside of School

Introduction

Many multilingual adolescents engage in a wide range of writing practices outside of school. Their out-of-school writing includes therapeutic journal or diary writing, instant messaging, social media writing (e.g., posting on Facebook, Twitter, Instagram), online community writing (e.g., posting on fan fiction sites), writing reviews on their favorite video games, drawing comic strips, submitting columns or editorials to local newspapers, and sharing self-made videos with a wide audience, among others. In addition, many immigrant or refugee adolescents, who often serve as critical linguistic and cultural resources in their families and local communities, engage in functional literacy required in their everyday lives (e.g., filling prescriptions, completing medical forms or documents, and composing complaint letters on behalf of their parents).

For all these writing activities, adolescent multilingual students tend to voluntarily and carefully choose languages (L1, L2, L3), mediums (digital, print), topics, forms, genres, styles, audience (private or public), and other possible mechanisms. While engaging in such writing practices, students seek to express themselves, communicate with people, construct and maintain social relationships with people around them, socialize with peers, pursue personal interests, create and maintain online communities, share information and experiences, make sense of their lives (immigrant life, teenage life), gain recognition from others, learn English, and explore identities. As such, adolescent multilingual students use out-of-school writing to accomplish personal, social, and academic goals in their daily lives.

This chapter provides a concise synthesis of research findings of adolescent multilingual students' writing in out-of-school contexts. It discusses the value and characteristics of out-of-school writing (e.g., self-initiated, voluntary, intentional, interest-driven, peer-driven, and multilingual) and illustrates ways in which adolescent multilingual students write, communicate, learn, and represent themselves through out-of-school writing across online, home, community, and workplace contexts.

Before Entering Conversations

Terms: Out-of-School Writing

Out-of-school writing, the focus of this chapter, is an umbrella term used in this book. It refers to self-initiated, self-sponsored, voluntary, and non-academic writing activities. Out-of-school writing is not defined or bound by a physical location or space, but it usually takes place outside of school and is not directly related to school work. For instance, students' homework for school has typically taken place in an out-of-school physical setting, but is considered an in-school, academic activity. Out-of-school writing is versatile in form, function, and purpose as noted above (e.g., journal writing, social media writing, poetry writing, comic drawing, and text-messaging). Literacy scholars have used various terms for similar meanings, such as "vernacular literacies" (Barton & Lee, 2012; de la Piedra, 2010; Grote, 2006), "unofficial literacy" (Maybin, 2007), "volitional writing" (Chamberlain, 2019), "extramural English" (Sundqivist & Olin-Scheller, 2013), "self-sponsored writing" (Yi & Angay-Crowder, 2018), and "informal writing" (Guzzetti & Gamboa, 2005). In this book, I use a term, out-of-school writing to encompass similar meanings of these terms.

A cautionary note that needs to be made is that a simple statement like "out-of-school writing is completely different or separate from in-school writing" is a myth. The in-school and out-of-school, place-driven dualism seems to be too simplistic to treat out-of-school writing because in-school and out-of-school writing practices often take place in almost a simultaneous and hybridized manner (Hultin & Westman, 2018), and out-of-school writing often permeates the boundaries of in-school writing practices (Grote, 2006). I acknowledge the false dichotomy of in-school and out-of-school writing (Alvermann & Moore, 2011; Vaughan, 2019) and do not endorse the dichotomous view. However, I still use terms, like "in-school" and "out-of-school" writing in this book because using them can help me explore the relationships (e.g., connections, continuities, and contradictions) between the two and develop a symbiotic approach to examining and cultivating the relationships (bidirectional, mutually beneficial) between the two. A more detailed discussion about the relationships between in-school and out-of-school writing is available in Chapter 5.

My Stance toward Out-of-School Writing

Before discussing adolescent multilingual students' out-of-school writing, I feel the need to share my stance first. My stance toward out-of-school writing practice and research is that we need to consider out-of-school writing *on its own*, not supplementary or complementary to academic writing. I do not want to examine and discuss out-of-school writing through a lens of academic writing development. Whenever I present my research on out-of-school writing at conferences or in public, I always receive a question of "So, how does out-of-school writing help improve academic writing?" Although I appreciate this question, I would rather ask a question, "How can researchers and educators create time, space, and opportunities that legitimate students' out-of-school writing practices, leverage them, and recognize adolescent multilingual students as writers?" I do not urge educators to simply apply out-of-school writing activities into classroom practices or redesign out-of-school writing activities to improve academic writing with the sole purpose of academic achievement. Instead, I argue that out-of-school writing is important *in and of itself.*

Status and Value of Out-of-School Writing

Unnoticed and Under-Valued in Research and Pedagogy

Since Shirley Brice Heath's classic research (1983), many studies, especially within the field of New Literacy Studies (NLS), have revealed that our children engage in a wide range of literacy practices in and outside of school. Yet, in both research and pedagogy, students' lived experiences with and their perspectives of writing beyond the boundaries of the classroom have generally been neglected. Simply put, out-of-school writing of students remain invisible and hidden (Daniel, 2019). In literacy research, school-based, academic literacy has been most powerful and important, and thus, out-of-school, non-academic literacy practices have been treated as less legitimate and less important (Hull & Schultz, 2002). Similarly, the L2 writing field has extensively researched academic writing and has paid much less attention to students' out-of-school writing practices as noted that the field "does not seem terribly interested in how individuals go about writing social, professional, or workplace genres" (Hyland, 2013, p. 426).

In pedagogy, many schools and teachers do not know much about students' out-of-school lives in general or out-of-school writing practices in particular. Their out-of-school writing experience and knowledge have remained unnoticed and undervalued in the classroom as they are less included in the curricula (Haddix, 2018). Teachers may not value students' out-of-school writing; some may treat it as "frivolous" and "leisure-time pursuits" (Black, 2009, p. 696). In fact, much of adolescent multilingual students' out-of-school writing is carried out in multiple languages (L1, L2, L3, and mixture of them), but unfortunately, such multiliterate experiences and capacities (knowledge, skills) are often overshadowed by the English-only and standard English ideologies and deficit perspectives of multilingual students (Enright, 2011).

Such views of out-of-school writing and English-only and standard English ideologies in research and pedagogy may influence students and parents to treat students' out-of-school literate lives as unimportant. While researching and working with many adolescent multilingual students, I have witnessed many times that some adolescent multilingual students do not see the value of their out-of-school writing experiences, knowledge, and skills even though some of their out-of-school writing is most meaningful and relevant to them (Yi, 2009; Yi, Kao, & Kang, 2017). They seem to have formed an idea that academic writing is always more validated and legitimized than self-initiated, out-of-school writing.

Why Out-of-School Writing Matters

Out-of-school writing matters, which is all about this chapter and this book. Here I briefly discuss why it matters. First and foremost, out-of-school writing is important to adolescent (multilingual) students. A youth writer in the after-school program, called "Writing Our Lives" (Haddix, 2018) described the role of out-of-school writing in life in the most powerful manner by noting "Writing is like *breathing*. I need it to survive" (p. 8). Through out-of-school writing practices, adolescent writers tend to negotiate their interests, identities, and other significant issues at the crossroads of linguistic, cultural, ethnic, and racial specificities among others. Out-of-school writing provides adolescents with more creative, meaningful, and expansive ways to communicate their ideas and experiences. In this regard, out-of-school writing may be a significant way to access opportunities in life (Haddix, 2018; Stewart, 2014), especially for students like "underground writers" (Haddix, 2018, p. 8) who do not engage in academic writing in school but extensively write outside of school. Overall, adolescent multilingual students use out-of-school writing for self-expression, personal enrichment, and academic requirements.

Equally important, in-depth understandings of multilingual students' out-of-school writing can make valuable contributions to literacy research and pedagogy. Research on their out-of-school writing has enabled researchers and practitioners to (1) have a better sense of students' full multiliterate capacities and multilingual repertoires (Enright, 2010), (2) challenge the "conventional notions of 'good' writing as individualistic, author-centric, monolingual, rigidly adherent to standard genres and conventions" (Black, 2009, p. 422), (3) reconceptualize what multilingual students can do with writing and how they learn and use writing in their daily lives, and (4) expand the continuum of literacy research.

Characteristics of Out-of-School Writing

Out-of-school writing practice shares some characteristics that make it significant, unique, and meaningful to students, teachers, and researchers. Here I explain its salient and defining characteristics in order to help readers better understand the nature of out-of-school writing of adolescent multilingual students.

Adolescent multilingual students' out-of-school writing tends to be self-directed *volitional practice*. Students voluntarily choose what and how to write when writing outside of school. Here, *a choice* is critical in out-of-school writing. They have autonomy to select everything that is involved in writing (e.g., content, genre, style, language, medium, audience, and purpose) without much constraints imposed by teachers. They can even spend extended period of time to develop ideas and finish writing.

In addition, out-of-school writing is an *intentional* act of representation and communication. For instance, some out-of-school writing practices are *interest-driven*. Such practices are driven by and linked to "fun and enjoyment" (Rothoni, 2017, p. 101). For instance, for Korean adolescent multilinguals, out-of-school writing was an enjoyable activity of choice (e.g., Soohee's diary writing, Joan's poetry writing, and Mike's online posting were clearly passion-filled, pleasurable writing for them) (Yi, 2009, 2010). Other practices are more *peer-driven* (e.g., exchanging notes and leaving comments on students' social networking sites), and thus students engage in out-of-school writing for "friendship-driven purposes" (Warschauer & Matuchniak, 2010, p. 192). Further, there are some practices, like video gaming, that can be both interest- and peer-driven as seen from Chinese adolescent ELs who regularly played online computer games for having fun and for socializing with peers (Li, Chiu, & Coady, 2014). Overall, such intentional, interest- and peer-driven writing practices amplify students' sense of authentic purpose and audience for writing. Both volitional and intentional characteristics of out-of-school writing suggest that out-of-school writing can be an agentive activity as adolescent students shape writing "to their own purposes, often in inventive ways" (Brandt & Clinton, 2002, p. 341).

Slightly differing from socially-oriented, interest- and peer-driven writing, some out-of-school writing is *private* and *personally-oriented*. Some may choose to keep their writing private by "remaining below the desk" (Gilmore, 1984, as cited in Chamberlain, 2019, p. 40). This is similar to the idea of the reflexive, "self-sponsored" writing. Self-sponsored writing (Emig, 1971) tends to focus on "the writer's thoughts and feelings occurring in his [her] experiences; the chief audience is the writer himself...; the style is tentative, personal, and exploratory" (p. 4).

Another significant characteristic is that out-of-school writing for multilingual students is *multilingual practices*. When writing outside of school, adolescent multilingual writers tend to employ more than one language. They may choose to write in their first or additional language(s) or in the mixture of the languages that they know. For multilingual students, the choice and use of languages is extremely important in their daily lives, which is perhaps the most significant difference from their monolingual English-speaking peers' literate lives. Importantly, students often demonstrate linguistic and cultural hybridity by leveraging multiple linguistic and cultural knowledge and experiences for their voluntary, out-of-school writing. For instance, Filipino British youth in London (Domingo, 2012, p. 184) voluntarily produced multilingual, multi-sourced, and hybrid texts (e.g., a rap song, "Pinoy Ako" [I am Filipino]) while navigating across the discourse communities of Filipino, British, hip hop, and youth pop culture.

Out-of-school writing is typically *not tested or graded*, which allows students to take risks and experiment with writing and languages, thereby producing more creative expressions (e.g., adolescent multilingual writers in fanfiction communities experimented with new genres of writing in Black, 2005). For out-of-school writing, educators do not necessarily need to "quantify writing outcomes" (Haddix, 2018, p. 10). This does not mean that they do not monitor the progress in writing. They do not tend to talk about writing development from the traditional sense of development, like test scores or high-stakes testing scores.

All the characteristics discussed so far also suggest that out-of-school writing practices, especially online practices are related to and driven by participatory culture. Participatory culture is defined as

> a culture with relatively low barriers to *artistic expression* and *civic engagement*, strong support for creating and *sharing* creations, and some type of informal mentorship whereby experienced participants pass along knowledge to novices. In a participatory culture, members also believe their contributions matter and feel some degree of *social connection with one another* (at the least, members care about others' opinions of what they have created).
>
> (Jenkins, 2009, p. xi)

Like the characteristics of participatory culture, many out-of-school writing activities are the means for expressing ideas and feelings, sharing with others, and maintaining social relationship with others, among others. This suggests that out-of-school writing is a social practice that allows multilingual students to engage in writing in a more authentic and inventive ways.

Out-of-School Writing, Technology, and Identity

"Literacy alone is no longer our business. Literacy and technology are. Or so they must become" (Selfe, 1999, p. 3). Today's students engage in much more out-of-school writing with digital technology than students were in the past. For instance, students 20 years ago might exchange print-based letters and notes with their friends, whereas students today may exchange instant messages and emails. Furthermore, individuals who were considered literate with a pen-and-paper may not meet the writing demands in the digital age. Among various types of out-of-school writing, digital multimodal writing is the most salient and popular kind for adolescent (multilingual) students (Tate, Warschauer, & Kim, 2019; Yi, Kao, & Kang, 2017). It is also something that they are likely to need so as to be a successful writer once they graduate from high school. In addition, digital multimodal writing outside of school facilitates adolescent multilingual students to express themselves and (re)construct their identities. Overall, out-of-school writing, identity construction, and the use of technology are inextricably linked for adolescent multilingual students.

Thus, this section focuses on discussing adolescent multilingual students' out-of-school writing practices in relation to technology use and identity construction. The first part focuses on reviewing earlier research on out-of-school writing in online communities; the second part centers on out-of-school writing practices on social networking sites (SNS). Although social networking sites are online communities in a broad sense, I decide to have a separate subsection on writing practices on SNS because they have unique characteristics and have been examined in more recent out-of-school writing research.

Out-of-School Writing in Online Communities

Some early studies examined adolescent multilingual students' out-of-school writing practices in *online community* contexts. Lam's (2000) exemplary study examined the online literacy practices of a Chinese immigrant teenager, named Almon, especially with respect to his L2 (English) literacy practices and identity formation. When Lam first met Almon at an after-school program in fall 1996, he expressed frustration over his insufficient English skills after living in the United States for 5 years and also worried about his future career. When Lam revisited the school to interview Almon after one year from the first encounter, she found that Almon had developed a "qualitatively different relationship" with the English language and writing (p. 468). After taking an introductory class on email and web searching skills, Almon became actively engaged in learning about the Internet (e.g., looking for online tutorials about how to make personal home pages and engage in online chatting). By fall 1997, he designed his personal home page on a Japanese popular singer, Ryoko Hirosue, chose his own pseudonym, *Mr. Children*, and called his home page *Mr. Children's Ryoko Page*. Almon engaged in various writing practices by adding information about the singer (e.g., a profile and biographic information) and communicating with people who left or viewed comments in "A Guess Book." In addition to the construction and maintenance of his home page, Almon also corresponded with a transnational group of peers around the world through online chatting and email. In doing so, he made a "visible improvement" in his writing in English and formed his "textual identity" (p. 467). To Almon, the Internet and online spaces opened up a new possibility of communication as well as ways to negotiate a self and to improve L2 literacy.

Another study by Lam (2004) powerfully showcased how the *bilingual chat room* provided two Chinese immigrant teens in the United States with a significant and meaningful context of L2 socialization and literacy practices. Two Chinese immigrant girls desired to improve speaking in English, but had limited opportunities to interact with their English-speaking peers, including English-speaking Chinese, in school. Both students initially explored the Internet for leisure purposes, but soon they learned about a chat room, called "Hong Kong (HK) chat room." At first, they did not join the chat room because they were afraid their English was not good enough to communicate, but they soon changed their minds to participate in order to make some friends and practice English. They typically spent three hours in the chat room every weekday and more during the weekends. Importantly, they preferred the HK chat room to American chat rooms like Yahoo because at the HK chat room they were able to meet with the wide range of English-speaking Chinese (mostly Chinese who had emigrated to different parts of the world) and shared some similar life experiences. While chatting online in a mixed-code variety of English (e.g., Romanized Cantonese, code-switching between English and Cantonese), they had built and maintained the relationships with other bilingual speakers of English and Cantonese as well as constructed a collective ethnic identity as bilingual Chinese emigrants. They finally began to see themselves as bilingual speakers rather than deficit non-native English speakers. Further, their digital literacy practices had positive effects on their positive identity construction.

Research by Black (2005, 2006) has also shown similar transformative effects of online, out-of-school writing practices. Her research participant, Tanaka, a Chinese-Canadian immigrant teenage girl, did not speak much English and had struggled with academic writing at first. She attempted to write fan fiction (fans of books, movies, comics, or TV shows develop new plots based on original characters and situations in it) in the online fanfiction site (www.fanfiction.net) in hopes that she would improve her writing skills and learn more about the Japanese animation and fanfiction culture. Only two months after joining the fanfiction site (i.e., 2.5 years after she moved from Shanghai to Canada), Tanaka engaged actively in writing online fan fiction stories, reading others' and carefully reviewing readers' feedback and comments on her stories. For instance, she wrote a story, *Crazy Love Letters* which significantly departed from the original storyline and consisted of 13 chapters, along with an epilogue. As one of her most popular fictions, it received over 1700 reader reviews over the period of one year she was writing it. Eventually Tanaka was able to "achieve the identity of a successful and wildly popular author" in the online community (Black, 2005, p. 173). Here she had developed an "online identity" as a confident multiliterate writer (p. 171).

Another related study is Yi's (2007, 2008) ethnographic study of multiliterate practices of Korean-American youth in an online community called *Welcome to Buckeye City* (WTBC), which was designed and maintained by a group of local friends. One of the most active participants and webmasters, Mike described WTBC as follows:

> It [Welcome to Buckeye City] is just a place where people, like teenagers, Korean teenagers, who live in the Buckeye area, like we know each other—a place we just can talk about anything like what happened today, or write a poem, write a story and upload pictures in it.... It's just a place that we can just hang out with friends, and we can talk about.... There is a page [section] you don't have to put your name, you can just put "anonymous," and you can say whatever you want in there. If you got problem, you can say it. People will reply.... I think it's just cool to write something and they reply to you. It's like fun. I think it's just a place you can relax and have fun.
>
> (Yi, 2008, p. 670)

As alluded above, this online community played a role as a "cyber-shelter for these teenagers" (Yi, 2007, p. 28) in which they could freely communicate and express themselves in any language (English, Korean, or the mixture of the two). Most of the WTBC members were generation 1.5 youth (Korean born and immigrated to the United States) or transnational youth (US born but lived back and forth between Korea and the United States) and were drawn to WTBC to share their perspectives and knowledge of the two languages, literacies, and cultures they had experienced. A wide range of texts were read, produced, and shared in this online community (e.g., self-introduction online posts, poems, quotes, reviews on music or movies, and survey questionnaires).

A unique out-of-school writing activity on WTBC and the focus of Yi's (2008) study was "relay writing" in which each member of the online community contributed a portion to an evolving story in a relayed manner (p. 670). For instance, the Captain in WTBC created a section, called "A Relay Novel," explained the rules for relay novel writing (e.g., one member could not write more than twice per week, and any member can write as "freely and creatively" as possible), and provided an initial theme, "beach." On the same day, one member posted the first episode for the relay novel by providing a vivid description of the background (beach) and introduced two main characters. He also added an author's commentary, and soon some members left review comments on the episode. As some members relayed the story, June known as a poet in the community contributed a poem that captured the theme of the novel, and Mike recommended background music for June's poem.

In addition to relay novel writing, there was another type of relay writing, called a "relay compliments activity" in which one WTBC member complimented another member (e.g., how they met, what kind of relationship they had established, and what good qualities they had), and the complimented member relayed the compliment process. This activity was drawn from a popular Korean TV show, "Let's Compliment." The TV show broadcasts a touching story about a person who has been doing good deeds for others in order to help them overcome any kind of hardship. This person who has been complimented for her or his service for others then introduces to the public another person who deserves public recognition and gifts. What is notable is that WTBC members transformed part of this TV show (heritage pop culture) into a kind of voluntary, out-of-school writing practice that worked for their online community. This relay compliment writing was very popular among the members because postings included very personal stories about the two members directly involved (i.e., the writer and the person being complimented) and accounts of memorable moments and events in the past, which revealed the personality and good qualities of the complimented person and the relationship between the two members. Overall, the complimenting member, the one complimented, and the rest of the members were all closely connected through this writing activity. This collaborative writing practice revolved around group production of texts, which quite differs from individual writing practices of multilingual teens in Lam's (2000, 2004) and Black's (2005, 2006) studies. This type of collaborative writing is compelling to researchers and practitioners because it shifts the focus from more individual production and authorship to collaborative, participatory forms of writing that are facilitated by emerging technologies (Black, 2009).

In summary, all these earlier studies on adolescent multilingual students' out-of-school writing practices in online communities were smaller-scale qualitative studies and primarily examined ways in which Asian adolescent immigrants engaged in out-of-school writing practices and constructed identities, such as textual, online, and transnational identities, through writing. On the other hand, these earlier studies on digital out-of-school writing relatively lack "strong representation from Latino youth" (Stewart, 2013, p. 31). Responding to this gap, more recent studies have investigated more diverse student populations as seen in the subsequent section. In addition, given that writing on social media and networking sites appears to be one of the most significant out-of-school writing for adolescents, the next section solely focuses on discussing writing practices on those sites.

Out-of-School Writing on Social Media and Social Networking Sites

Since the launch of social media and social networking sites (SNS) (e.g., MySpace, Facebook) in the mid-2000s, the use of SNS has become everyday practice to many young people. In the literacy field, more recent studies on out-of-school writing have documented writing engagement and identity construction on social media and social networking sites (e.g., Facebook, Twitter, and YouTube). Social network sites are defined as

> Web-based services that allow individuals to (1) construct a public or semi-public profile within a bounded system, (2) articulate a list of other users with whom they share a connection, and (3) view and traverse their list of connections and those made by others within the system.
>
> (Boyd & Ellison, 2008, p. 211)

It is anecdotally well-known and empirically documented that contemporary teens are connected to the Internet daily and write online extensively (Galvin & Greenhow, 2020). For instance, 73% of teens use several social media daily (Rideout & Robb, 2018), and 89% of teens are connected to the Internet daily (45% for constant connection and 44% for logging on several times each day) (Anderson & Jiang, 2018). Teens' use of social media has more than doubled since 2012 (Rideout & Robb, 2018, as cited in Galvin & Greenhow, 2020, p. 57). Given these, writing on the social networking sites is perhaps the most frequent out-of-school writing for adolescent multilingual students. Educational researchers have shown that social networking sites can "uniquely serve the purposes of youth who have experienced immigration" (Stewart, 2013, p. 31). They provide students with opportunities for (1) more engaging and authentic writing (Galvin & Greenhow, 2020), (2) identity exploration and construction (Davies, 2012; Schreiber, 2015), and (3) authentic social interaction (Padgett & Curwood, 2016).

Among many social networking sites, Facebook, the largest social media platform worldwide, is most widely examined in the fields of L2 writing and literacy studies. Despite the extensive use of SNS outside of school, most of studies on Facebook in TESOL and applied linguistics conducted in the *classroom* contexts and/or about *college/adult* learners (e.g., Barrot, 2021; Chen, 2013; DePew, 2011; Lee & Ranta, 2014). Similarly, for adolescent students, a few studies took place in the ESL classroom contexts. For instance, Vanek, King, and Bigelow (2018) examined the possibilities of using Facebook to support learning in a high school ESL class of recently arrived migrants in the United States. These English-learning adolescents engaged with writing and the critical text analysis on Facebook posts. More recently, examining five adolescent ELs' use of digital technology in the ESL classroom in an American high school, Andrei (2019) found these teens engaged in some voluntary, digital writing practices for entertainment purposes, including texting (using Facebook, Snapchat, WhatsApp, and text application from phone carrier), posting on Facebook and Instagram, watching videos and cartoons, Google searching, listening to music, taking picture, and so forth.

Despite the ubiquitous use of social media and SNS among today's teens, there is little research on adolescent multilingual students' engagement with SNS outside of school. In this sense, McLean's (2010) and Stewart's (2013) studies are worth attention here because both demonstrate how adolescent multilingual students participated in SNS in their daily lives.

McLean (2010) examined how a 15-year-old Caribbean American adolescent girl, named Zeek, used online digital technology and digital literacies to negotiate her identity. As an avid member of Facebook and MySpace, she posted and shared photos, comments, songs, and hyperlinks that reflect her ties to the Caribbean and the United States. While adapting to the United States, she stayed connected to her native country and identity. Her digital literacy practices reflected her identities and group affiliation. In particular, digital and multimodal texts (e.g., the Trinidad and Tobago national flag, pictures of favorite Caribbean destinations) on her Facebook profile and wall represented her "ethnic group membership" and her efforts to reflect and maintain "cultural identities" (p. 19). Overall, the digital world allowed her to engage in literacy and identity-making practices.

Similarly, Stewart's (2013) study also investigated the Facebook use of four-newcomer high school ELs in the United States. They were transnational, emergent bilinguals, and proud Latina/o, but they were labeled as at-risk at school, struggling academically. Some Facebook practices in which they engaged included exchanging messages and pictures of themselves (e.g., wearing a Guatemalan soccer jersey), their friends, and family members on a daily basis; changing their profile pictures; posting on their walls; posting and watching videos (e.g., graduation videos); and updating information pages, among others. These newcomers, like Zeek in McLean (2010), used Facebook to sustain a tie to their home countries (El Salvador, Mexico, Guatemala), maintain their Latina/o identities, and acquire English, which collectively contributed to their transnational identity construction. Importantly, Facebook became an important space for them to *develop their English* (e.g., Alejandra wrote longer phrases in English on Facebook than for school). Three of the participants reported that they rarely talked to "americanos" in school, as one stated, "Here in school I really don't have American friends, so I have them on Facebook" (p. 37). Celia, one of the participants, asked Alejandra to post messages to her in English so that she could practice English. Overall, through Facebook writing outside of school, these transnational newcomers learned how to "communicate in multimodal ways in two languages and multiple registers with people of different backgrounds across multiple borders, challenging the at-risk label" (p. 11).

Finally, Kim's (2018) study, focusing on digital translanguaging practices of a Korean transnational youth living in the United States, illustrates the participant's digital multimodal literacy engagement outside school. For instance, the participant, Jenna created four video clips, including some for her extended family in Korea (e.g., *New Year's Greeting, Happy Birthday Grandpa*). Further, she hung out with her online "friends" at a social media site, *Google+* which served as an online affinity community where Jenna interacted with other translocal and transnational peers. They often shared their lives' challenges and experiences as transnational adolescents (e.g., school life and peer relationships), exchanged information about different educational systems, such as testing and school subjects, and made comments on their friends' updates on profile, photo, or images. In addition, some serious sociopolitical topics were discussed as well. Jenna wrote "a tribute" to many Korean civilians who protested and lost their lives to fight for democracy in the 1980s. Here, digital communication and writing on a social media site facilitated "even greater interactive opportunities for the writer to link diverse voices, cultural resources, and semiotic modes" (Kim, 2018, p. 50), which is exceptionally prominent among transnational youth.

Summary of Out-of-School Writing, Technology, and Identity

All these studies on adolescent multilingual students' digital out-of-school writing indicate that online and digital spaces (e.g., fan fiction communities, local online communities, and social networking communities) serve as a contact zone that incorporates multiple languages, literacies, cultures (e.g., native, host, transnational, online, and popular culture), and non-linguistics resources (images and sounds), as well as enables adolescent students to engage in rich, authentic, and interactive writing activities. Here it is especially important to highlight that all the studies have collectively pointed out the important role that a community or an affinity group played in students' literate lives. While students are becoming active or even peripheral members in online communities, they engage in writing activities to varying degrees, develop a great sense of audience and purpose, become apprenticed for writing development, foster interpersonal relationships/social networks, and negotiate their multiple identities and memberships across multiple communities. Emerging technologies, voluntary nature of out-of-school writing, and identity construction are all intertwined, which facilitates students' writing and identity-(re)making practices.

Out-of-School Writing at Home, Community, and Workplace

As discussed in the previous section, adolescent multilingual students' out-of-school writing practices are connected to their peers and more dependent on emerging technologies because adolescents, while showing more autonomy and independence from their parents, use writing to socialize and communicate with people, pursue their interests, and (re)negotiate multiple identities. A relatively small number of studies (e.g., Cruickshank, 2004, de la Piedra, 2010; Godina, 2004; Joo, 2009) have documented adolescent multilingual students' out-of-school writing at home, (ethnic) community, and workplace, which is the focus of this section. While the previous section focuses more on the use of emerging technologies for out-of-school writing and identity construction, this section focuses more on print-based writing and literacy practices that are connected to students' immigrant life experiences and their participations in local communities and workplaces.

de la Piedra (2010) documented *vernacular literacies* in which 14 newly arrived Mexican immigrant youth in Texas engaged at home. One of significant vernacular literacies at home was that some students translated and explained significant information around legal documents to other families, especially newly arrived families. They played a significant role as a "literacy mediator and translator" (p. 578). Another unique literacy practice showcased at home was, in some households, the adolescents wanted to bring literacy practices learned at school to home. For instance, some read the texts from school in English to their parents or siblings (e.g., reciting poems in English), and others taught their parents some strategies to help younger siblings with school assignments. As such, these adolescent immigrant students engaged in functional writing and literacy practices (literacy brokering and sibling/parent tutoring) to help their immigrant parents and families.

Cruickshank's (2004) research is worth attention because it is one of the few studies that examined adolescent multilingual students' out-of-school writing in Arabic-speaking families. From the longitudinal ethnographic study with the four teenagers and their families emigrating from Lebanon to Sydney, Australia, Cruickshank found that multilingual teenagers engaged in various out-of-school writing and literacy activities at home, including writing letters to their relatives in Lebanon, writing notes explaining school absence for themselves or their siblings, writing homework for their Arabic community school, and memorizing verses of Quran. Similar to many immigrant family literacy practices, their writing and literacy practices at home took place for the needs of daily life, entertainment, communication, education, and religion.

In addition to the writing practices at home, some multilingual teens engage in writing in a local community. In Mariana Pacheco's study (2015), Sara, a 9th grade bilingual student, participated in a community-based teen newsroom community. As a novice teen journalist, she started engaging in summarizing newspapers, encyclopedia, Internet, magazines, and textbook sources. She sometimes wrote book reviews, editorials, and special interest articles. She experienced significant challenges with writing in English during more than the first two years, but the writing conferences among Sara and editorial staff members had guided and supported her writing. As such, while engaging in everyday newsroom literacy practices, Sara had been apprenticed into the newsroom community.

Finally, adolescent multilingual students also engaged in workplace writing and literacy practices, although their out-of-school writing in workplaces has been underexplored. One notable exception is Stewart's (2014) study about four newcomer Latina/o adolescents' workplace literacies in the United States. Interestingly, all the participating students worked for about 35–40 hours per week (e.g., work at the sandwich shop), although none had ever had jobs in their home countries. Their workplace literacy practices included reading labels, translating, speaking to co-workers, and filling the orders. Importantly, such practices enabled them to (a) acquire English, (b) create a space to succeed, which led them "to be someone," and (c) support themselves financially (p. 357). In terms of English acquisition, 100% of their "americano" friends were their former or current-then co-workers, and thus they had much more opportunities to practice English in their workplaces than in school. These adolescent multilingual students rarely had meaningful opportunities to speak English and interact with English-speaking peers in school. Yet, in their workplaces, they had to speak and write English with their co-workers, customers, and managers to communicate and accomplish given tasks.

Another reason for the importance of workplace literacies for these adolescents was that although all might have felt unsuccessful in school, at work they all carved out a space where they could succeed. For instance, Valeria made more money than any other non-managerial staff. Alejandra was in a position to train new employees because she was the only person who knew about the kitchen and the front at the Sandwich shop and she had become very important to the manager. Celia was incredibly successful at El Taco Loco by translating between English-speaking and Spanish-speaking people (co-workers and customers) and had received a raise.

Workplace literacies are also critical in terms of supporting themselves financially. For these students, making money meant supporting themselves. Some had to self-support, and others had to send some money to their families in home countries. In addition, saving money meant saving for futures (e.g., college). As such, their workplaces were extremely important spaces where many writing and literacy practices took place.

Concluding Remarks about Adolescent Multilingual Writing Outside of School

This chapter surveys a wide range of out-of-school writing practices in which adolescent multilingual students engage for various purposes. It gives researchers and practitioners valuable insights into adolescent students' ways of experiencing writing and literacy beyond the classroom. Throughout this comprehensive survey, I explicitly and implicitly have made several arguments. First, we should respect adolescent multilingual students' self-initiated, voluntary out-of-school writing while acknowledging that it is important *in and of itself.* Although out-of-school writing, frequently done unnoticed, is often hidden in the shallows of school expectations, many multilingual adolescents engage in rich, versatile, and meaningful writing outside of school, which challenges deficit views of adolescent multilingual students and their writing. Second, researchers and practitioners need to rethink about "what counts as writing (literacy)" for adolescent multilingual students in the 21st century. Writing for young people is beyond persuasive essays or research papers (the most frequent types of writing in school). The richness and diversity of their engagement with writing outside of school call for expanding the notion of what counts as writing. Third, it is critical to consider the role of out-of-school writing and literacy practices in the current and future lives of adolescent multilingual students. I believe the discussions about these three specific arguments will enable researchers and practitioners to broaden the perspectives of adolescent writing and literacy as well as to conduct more equitable teaching for adolescent students.

References

Alvermann, D., & Moore, D. (2011). Questioning the separation of in-school from out-of-school contexts for literacy learning: An interview with Donna E. Alvermann. *Journal of Adolescent & Adult Literacy, 55*(2), 156–158. https://doi.org/10.1002/JAAL.00019

Anderson, M., & Jiang, J. (2018, May 31). Teens, social media & technology 2018. Pew Research Center. https://www.pewresearch.org/internet/2018/05/31/teens-social-media-technology-2018/

Andrei, E. (2019). Adolescent English learners' use of digital technology in the classroom. *The Educational Forum, 83*(1), 102–120. https://doi.org/10.1080/00131725.2018.1478474

Barrot, J. S. (2021).Effects of Facebook-based e-portfolio on ESL learners' writing performance. *Language, Culture & Curriculum, 34*(1), 95–111. https://doi.org/10.1080/07908318.2020.1745822

Barton, D., & Lee, C. K. M. (2012). Redefining vernacular literacies in the age of web 2.0. *Applied Linguistics, 33*(3), 282–298. https://doi.org/10.1093/applin/ams009

Black, R. W. (2005). Access and affiliation: The literacy and composition practices of English language learners in an online fanfiction community. *Journal of Adolescent and Adult Literacy, 49*(2), 118–128. https://doi.org/10.1598/JAAL.49.2.4

Black, R. W. (2006). Language, culture, and identity in online fanfiction. *E-Learning, and Digital Media, 3*(2), 170–184. https://doi.org/10.2304/elea.2006.3.2.170

Black, R. W. (2009). Online fan fiction, global identities, and imagination. *Research in the Teaching of English, 43*(4), 397–425.

Boyd, D., & Ellison, N. B. (2008). Social network sites definition, history, and scholarship. *Journal of Computer-Mediated Communication, 13*(1), 210–230. https://doi.org/10.1111/j.1083-6101.2007.00393.x

Brandt, D., & Clinton, K. (2002). Limits of the local: Expanding perspective on literacy as a social practice. *Journal of Literacy Research, 34*(3), 337–356. https://doi.org/10.1207/s15548430jlr3403_4

Chamberlain, L. (2019). Places, spaces and local customs: Honouring the private worlds of out- of-school text creation. *Literacy, 51*(1), 39–45. https://doi.org/10.1111/lit.12154

Chen, H. (2013). Identity practices of multilingual writers in social networking spaces. *Language Learning and Technology, 17*(2), 143–170.

Cruickshank, K. (2004). Literacy in multilingual contexts: Change in teenagers' reading and writing. *Language & Education, 18*(6), 459–473. https://doi.org/10.1080/09500780408666895

Daniel, S. M. (2019). Writing our identities for successful endeavors: Resettled refugee youth look to the future. *Journal of Research in Childhood Education, 33*(1), 71–83. https://doi.org/10.1080/02568543.2018.1531448

Davies, J. (2012). Facework on Facebook as a new literacy practice. *Computers & Education, 59*, 19–29. https://doi.org/10.1016/j.compedu.2011.11.007

de la Piedra, M. T. (2010). Adolescent worlds and literacy practices on the United States–Mexico border. *Journal of Adolescent & Adult Literacy, 53*(7), 575–584. https://doi.org/10.1598/JAAL.53.7.5

DePew, K. E. (2011). Social media at academia's periphery: Studying multilingual developmental writers' Facebook composing strategies. *Reading Matrix: An International Online Journal, 11*(1), 54–75.

Domingo, M. (2012). Linguistic layering: Social language development in the context of multimodal design and digital technologies. *Learning, Media, & Technology, 37*(2), 177–197. https://doi.org/10.1080/17439884.2012.670645

Emig, J. (1971). *The composing processes of twelfth graders.* Urbana, IL: National Council of Teachers of English.

Enright, K. A. (2010). Academic literacies and adolescent learners: English for subject-matter secondary classroom. *TESOL Quarterly, 44*(4), 804–810. https://doi: 10.5054/tq.2010.237336

Enright, K. A. (2011). Language and literacy for a new mainstream. *American Educational Research Journal, 48*(1), 80–118. https://doi.org/10.3102%2F0002831210368989

Galvin, S., & Greenhow, C. (2020). Writing on social media: A review of research in the high school classroom. *TechTrends, 64*, 57–69. https://doi.org/10.1007/s11528-019-00428-9

Gilmore, P. (1984). Research currents: Assessing sub-rosa skills in children's language. *Language Arts, 61*(4), 384–391.

Godina, H. (2004). Contradictory literacy practices of Mexican-background students: An ethnography from the rural Midwest. *Bilingual Research Journal, 28*(2), 153–180.

Grote, E. (2006). Challenging the boundaries between school-sponsored and vernacular literacies: Urban indigenous teenage girls writing in an "at risk" programme. *Language and Education, 20*, 478–492. https://doi.org/10.2167/le659.0

Guzzetti, B., & Gamboa, M. (2005). Online journaling: The informal writings of two adolescent girls. *Research in the Teaching of English, 40*(2), 168–206.

Haddix, M. M. (2018). Writing our lives: Preparing teachers to teach 21st century writers in and out of school. In K. Zenkov & K. E. Pytash (Eds.), *Clinical experiences in teacher education* (pp. 137–152). New York: Routledge.

Heath, S. B. (1983). *Ways with words: Language, life, and work in communities and classrooms.* Cambridge, UK: Cambridge University Press.

Hull, G. Y., & Schultz, K. (Eds.). (2002). *School's out!: Bridging out-of-school literacies with classroom practice.* New York: Teachers College Press.

Hultin, E., & Westman, M. (2018). The reuse of semiotic resources in third-year children's writing of sub-genres. *Journal of Early Childhood Literacy, 18*(4), 518–544. https://doi.org/10.1177/1468798416685768

Hyland, K. (2013). Second language writing: The manufacture of a social fact. *Journal of Second Language Writing, 22*(4), 426–427. http://dx.doi.org/10.1016/j.jslw.2013.08.001

Jenkins, H. (2009). *Confronting the challenges of participatory culture: Media education for the 21st century.* Cambridge, MA: The MIT Press.

Joo, H. (2009). Literacy practices and heritage language maintenance: The case of Korean- American immigrant adolescents. *Journal of Asian Pacific Communication, 19*(1), 76–99. https://doi.org/10.1075/japc.19.1.05joo

Kim, S. (2018). "It was kind of a given that we were all multilingual": Transnational youth identity work in digital translanguaging. *Linguistics & Education, 43,* 39–52. https://doi.org/10.1016/j.linged.2017.10.008

Lam, W. S. E. (2000). L2 literacy and the design of the self: A case study of a teenager writing on the Internet. *TESOL Quarterly, 34*(3), 457–482. https://doi.org/10.2307/3587739

Lam, W. S. E. (2004). Second language socialization in a bilingual chat room: Global and local considerations. *Language learning & Technology, 8*(3), 44–65. https://doi.org/10125/43994

Lee, K., & Ranta, L. (2014). Facebook: Facilitating social access and language acquisition for international students?. *TESL Canada Journal, 31*(2), 22–50. https://doi.org/10.18806/tesl.v31i2.1175

Li, Z., Chiu, C., & Coady, M. R. (2014). The transformative power of gaming literacy. In. H. R. Gerber, S. S. Abrams (Eds.), *Bridging literacies with videogames* (pp. 129–152). Boston, MA: Sense Publisher.

Maybin, J. (2007). Literacy under and over the desk: Oppositions and heterogeneity. *Language & Education, 21*(6), 515–530. https://doi.org/10.2167/le720.0

McLean, C. A. (2010). A space called home: An immigrant adolescent's digital literacy practices. *Journal of Adolescent & Adult Literacy, 54*(1), 13–22. https://doi.org/10.1598/JAAL.54.1.2

Pacheco, M. (2015). Bilingualism-as-participation: Examining adolescents' bi(multi)lingual literacies across out-of-school and online contexts. In D. Molle, E. Sato, T. Boals & C. A. Hedgspeth (Eds.), *Multilingual learners and academic literacies: Sociocultural contexts of literacy development* (pp. 135–165). New York: Routledge.

Padgett, E. R., & Curwood, J. S. (2016). A figment of their imagination: Adolescent poetic literacy in an online affinity space. *Journal of Adolescent & Adult Literacy, 11,* 397–407. https://doi.org/10.1002/jaal.453

Rideout, V., & Robb, M. B. (2018). *Social media, social life: Teens reveal their experiences.* San Francisco, CA: Common Sense Media.

Rothoni, A. (2017). The interplay of global forms of pop culture and media in teenagers' 'interest-driven' everyday literacy practices with English in

Greece. *Linguistics & Education*, *38*, 92–103. https://doi.org/10.1016/j. linged.2017.03.001

Schreiber, B. R. (2015). "I am what I am": Multilingual identity and digital translanguaging. *Language, Learning & Technology*, *19*(3), 69–87. https://doi. org/10125/44434

Selfe, C. L. (1999). *Technology and literacy in the twenty-first century: The importance of paying attention*. Carbondale, IL: Southern Illinois University Press.

Stewart, M. A. (2013). Living here, yet being there: Facebook as a transnational space for newcomer Latina/o adolescents. *Tapestry*, *5*(1), 28–43.

Stewart, M. A. (2014). Social networking, workplace, and entertainment literacies: The out-of-school literate lives of newcomer adolescent immigrants. *Literacy Research & Instruction*, *53*(4), 347–371. https://doi.org/10.1080/1938 8071.2014.931495

Sundqivist, P., & Olin-Scheller, C. (2013). Classroom vs. extramural English: Teachers dealing with demotivation. *Language and Linguistics Compass*, *7*(6), 329–338. https://doi.org/10.1111/lnc3.12031

Tate, T. P., Warschauer, M., & Kim, Y. G. (2019). Learning to compose digitally: The effect of prior computer use and keyboard activity on NAEP writing. *Reading and Writing*, *32*, 2059–2082. https://doi.org/10.1007/ s11145-019-09940-z

Vanek, J., King, K., & Bigelow, M. (2018). Social presence and identity: Facebook in an English language classroom. *Journal of Language, Identity & Education*, *17*(4), 236–254. https://doi.org/10.1080/15348458.2018.1442223

Vaughan, A. (2019). Conceptualizing scholarship on adolescent out-of-school writing toward more equitable teaching and learning: A literature review. *Journal of Adolescent & Adult Literacy*, *63*(5), 529–537. https://doi.org/ 10.1002/jaal.1009

Warschauer, M., & Matuchniak, T. (2010). New technology and digital worlds: Analyzing evidence of equity in access, ese, and outcomes. *Review of Research in Education*, *34*(1), 179–225. https://doi.org/10.3102/0091732X09349791

Yi, Y. (2007). Engaging literacy: A biliterate student's composing practices beyond school. *Journal of Second Language Writing*, *16*, 23–39. https://doi. org/10.1016/j.jslw.2007.03.001

Yi. Y. (2008). Relay writing in an adolescent online community. *Journal of Adolescent & Adult Literacy*, *51*(8), 670–680. https://doi.org/10.1598/ JAAL.51.8.6

Yi, Y. (2009). Adolescent literacy and identity construction among 1.5 generation students: From a transnational perspective. *Journal of Asian Pacific Communication*, *19*(1), 100–129. https://doi.org/10.1075/japc.19.1.06yi

Yi, Y. (2010). Adolescent multilingual writer's transitions between in- and out-of- school writing practices. *Journal of Second Language Writing*, *19*, 17–32. https://doi.org/10.1016/j.jslw.2009.10.001

Yi, Y., & Angay-Crowder, T. (2018). Self-sponsored writing. In J. I. Liontas (Ed.), *The TESOL encyclopedia of English language teaching*. Hoboken, NJ: Wiley. https://doi.org/10.1002/9781118784235.eelt0521

Yi, Y., Kao, C., & Kang, J. (2017). Digital multimodal composing practices of adolescent English language learners in an after-school program. In S. Rilling & M. Dantas-Whitney (Eds.), *TESOL voices: Insider accounts of classroom life* (pp. 49–55). Alexandria, VA: TESOL Press.

Yi, Y., King, N., & Safriani, A. (2017). Re-conceptualizing assessment of digital multimodal literacy. *TESOL Journal, 8*(4), 878–885. https://doi.org/10.1002/tesj.354

4 Adolescent Multilingual Writing in School

Introduction

Adolescent multilingual students' writing experiences and practices tend to transcend across physical, territorial boundaries (e.g., classroom, home, church, community centers, and social networks); however, this chapter focuses on discussing issues in school-sponsored, academic writing so that readers can better understand the nature of academic writing practices, development, and contexts in comparison with self-initiated, out-of-school writing practices discussed in the previous chapter (Chapter 3). I begin by defining terms, such as academic language, literacy, and writing in English-medium institutional contexts and then discuss major research findings about (1) types of writing activities in the classroom, (2) content area writing, (3) writing processes, strategies, and products, (4) factors influencing academic writing development, and (5) identity and technology. Discussions and research syntheses in this chapter collectively can help readers better understand the nature of academic writing for adolescent multilingual students.

Key Terms

Although researchers and practitioners talk about academic writing and writing development, they may conceptualize them in different manners. Before I discuss issues of adolescent multilingual students' academic writing, I need to explain some key terms and concepts, such as academic language, literacy, and writing, as well as writing development and writing contexts.

Academic Language

It seems there is no single or simple definition of academic language (see Anstrom et al. (2010) for a comprehensive review on academic language), but educational researchers have defined it as

- "the language that is used by teachers and students for the purpose of acquiring new knowledge and skills … imparting new information, describing abstract ideas, and developing students' conceptual understanding" (Chamot & O'Malley, 1994, p. 40),
- "language associated with the academic discourse of the various school subjects" (Fillmore & Snow, 2000, p. 7),
- "the language used in school, in writing, in public, in formal settings" (Snow & Uccelli, 2009, p. 112),
- "[academic language is] functional for getting things done at school, varying as it is used in different subject areas and for different purposes, but requiring that children use language in new ways to learn and to display knowledge about what they have learned in ways that will be valued" (Schleppegrell, 2012, p. 410).

Similarly, Scarcella (2003) uses a term, *academic English* and defines it as "a variety or register of English used in professional books and characterized by the linguistic features associated with academic disciplines" (p. 9). All these definitions imply that academic language is required for *doing well* in school, but some may argue that these definitions tend to "treat mastery of academic language as an end itself rather than a means to the achievement of a variety of ends that are not purely linguistic" (Haneda, 2014, p. 128).

Recently, educational researchers have argued for the expanded notion of academic language (Bunch, 2006; Haneda, 2014; Villalva, 2006). For instance, Bunch (2006, p. 284), while challenging the dichotomy between "academic" language and "conversational" language (often called social language), argues that both are two different academic uses of language that are vital to completing academic tasks. In addition, Villalva (2006) reframes academic English by situating it within the notions of multiple literacies. She argues for considering "classroom language use as both product and process at the intersection of a variety of contexts within and outside of school" (p. 122). These expanded definitions, which this book is more aligned with, seem to place the notion of academic language on a continuum, treating it in relation to other kinds of languages and literacies.

Academic Literacy and Literacies

Of some definitions of academic literacy, the one from *Adolescent English Language Learners Literacy Advisory Panel* directly addresses adolescent multilingual students. The panel developed the definition of "academic literacy" as it

- includes reading, writing, and oral discourse for school,
- varies from subject to subject,
- requires knowledge of multiple genres of text, purposes for text use, and text media,
- is influenced by students' literacies in contexts outside of school,
- is influenced by students' personal, social, and cultural experiences (Short & Fitzsimmons, 2007, p. 8).

Although this definition seems to be comprehensive, recent scholarship has adopted the plural form of a word, literacies to emphasize the multiplicity and situatedness of academic literacy practices while conceptualizing literacy as social and cultural practices (e.g., Enright, 2010; Lea & Street, 2006). These scholars consider academic literacies one of multiple literacies in which adolescent multilingual students engage in their daily lives. According to Mariana Pacheco (2015), academic literacies are "situated, dynamic, contextualized, and mutually constituted across the normative tasks and activities that co-participants accomplish in different spaces, including classrooms" (p. 137). Furthermore, Molle, Sato, Boals, and Hedgspeth (2015) describe academic literacies as "multimodal, multilingual, multicultural; open, critical, creative; purposeful, strategic, pragmatic; developmental; inter/intra personal; and fluid, lived, messy" (p. 4).

Academic Writing

Academic writing refers to school-sponsored, official, and conventional writing for academic purposes. As noted above, the perspectives of academic literacy or literacies encompass the complex and multiple nature of academic literacy practices; however, I decide to use a term, academic *writing* in this book. As I noted in Chapter 1, when educators use a word, "literacy," it seems to automatically refer to or emphasize reading over writing. In educational research and pedagogy, writing has been considered a "neglected R" among three Rs (reading, writing, and arithmetic) (National Commission on Writing in America's Schools and Colleges, 2003; Sessions, Kang, & Womack, 2016). Thus, *academic writing* rather than academic literacy is used in this book for a more focused and intentional attention to the discussion of writing.

Writing Development

Writing development can be understood differently depending on different perspectives. For instance, cognitive researchers may argue that the increase of accuracy of using certain linguistic features means writing development, whereas some sociocultural researchers may argue that when students have constructed writer identities, their writing has developed. Writing development cannot be defined in a single or simple manner. Instead, Graham (2019) summarizes what research has revealed about writing development in his review paper:

- Writing development is further shaped by a variety of processes operating at the individual level.
- Writing development is also shaped through instruction.
- Regardless of the processes that shape students' growth as writers, writing development is variable, with no single path or end point.
- Writing development influences and is influenced by development in speech, reading, learning, emotions, identity, a sense of efficacy, and collective actions.
- Writing development is influenced by gender, family wealth, culture, neurological functioning, and genetic factors (pp. 286–287).

In addition to these aspects of writing development, a *multilingual* aspect is especially critical to understand writing development of multilingual writers. Multilingual writers tend to develop writing in two or more languages, unlike monolingual writers who develop writing in one language, and thus looking into their writing development from a monolingual perspective (e.g., examining their writing development only in English) offers a partial view of writing development. Thus, some L2 writing scholars (Gentil, 2011; Kibler, 2014) have called for more research and pedagogical attention to multilingual students' writing development in two or more languages, keeping students' multi-year trajectories of writing development in mind.

Writing Contexts

The contexts of writing are one of the most significant factors that influence the nature and quality of student writing (Wilcox, Yagelski, & Yu, 2014). According to Schultz and Fecho (2000), writing contexts

include "the genres, the purposes for writing, and the audiences –
both real and imagined- for the text. In addition, the contexts account
for the particular task and the rhetorical conventions that shape the
task" (p. 56). This explanation of writing contexts addresses micro-
level contextual factors, but writing contexts need to be understood
at both macro and micro levels. Some macro-level contextual factors
include education policies and language ideologies influencing writing practice and development. For instance, standard-driven testing
as well as English-only and standard English ideologies tend to lead
the narrowing of the curriculum and standardization of instruction,
which ultimately impacts the writing experiences and opportunities of
adolescent multilingual writers in the classroom (Enright, 2010).

Types of Writing Activities in the Classroom

Several national studies about writing instruction in middle and high
schools in the United States give researchers and practitioners valuable
insights into the types of writing activities and assignments in which
adolescent students (including both multilingual and native English-
speaking students) actually engage for academic purposes. A decade
ago, a national survey of randomly selected 361 teachers across the
three content areas (language arts, social studies, and science) from
American *high school* classrooms (Kiuhara, Graham, & Hawken, 2009)
revealed that the writing activities that these teachers assigned generally involved "little analysis and interpretation" (p. 136), and almost a
half of the participating teachers (47%) did not even assign at least one
multi-paragraph writing homework once per month. Although multi-
paragraph writing activities did not frequently take place, researchers identified the most frequent eight writing assignments that require
multi-paragraph writing, such "five-paragraph essay, persuasive
essay, research paper, short story, book report, biography, autobiogra-
phy, and stage/screenplay," with a five-paragraph essay and a persuasive essay most popular among them (p. 142).

More recently, Graham et al. (2014) conducted a national study
about *middle school* writing in the United States. From the data of
285 randomly selected 6th to 8th grade teachers, 30 different types
of writing activities were identified. The four most common writing
activities include "short answer responses, note taking, completing
worksheets, and writing in response to material read" (p. 1040). Over
50% of teachers asked their students to engage in one of these common writing activities at least once a week. Interestingly, some writing
activities like "blogs, emails, plays, business letters, autobiographies,
biographies, and lab reports" were *never assigned* by most teachers.

Another national study in a larger scale (Applebee & Langer, 2011) explored writing instruction in both middle and high schools in the United States. They gathered the data from visits to 260 classrooms in 20 middle and high schools in 5 states (California, Kentucky, Michigan, New York, and Texas); interviews with 220 teachers/administrators and 138 students in these schools; a national survey of 1520 randomly selected teachers; and 8542 writing assignments from the 138 student participants. The analysis of such a large set of data revealed that the adolescent students wrote more for their English (language arts) classes than any other subject (i.e., math, science, and social studies), but they wrote more for their other subjects combined than they did for English, which implies that adolescent students experienced academic writing across the curriculum. In terms of extended writing (defined as writing a paragraph or more in this study), only 7.7% of the observed class time was devoted to extended writing; only 19% of the assignments collected included writing of a paragraph or more. Less than 1% of the writing assignments during a 9-week observation period required students to produce three pages or more in length.

Collectively, these national studies of academic writing in middle and high schools in the United States teach researchers and practitioners that adolescent students are asked to engage in quite various types of academic writing for different purposes (e.g., writing to understand their reading, to inform, and to persuade); however, writing in general did not occur frequently.

Unlike the large-scale, quantitative national studies discussed so far, Lawrence, Galloway, Yim, and Lin (2013) conducted a qualitative study of four adolescent students' writing experiences across content classes in the American middle school. Researchers found 17 different genres in which the participants engaged across disciplines (i.e., English language arts, math, science, and social studies), the greatest range in English language arts (ELA). Three most popular genres in ELA were "notes from textbook or class" (17.7%), "journal" (13.7%), and "summary" (12.9%), which are all non-analytical writing. Related to this finding, one striking and troubling finding was the lack of *analytical writing* tasks and activities. For instance, approximately only 15% of the writing from ELA and math classes could be considered analytical writing, and no example of analytical writing was found from the social studies classroom.

Another related study (Llosa, Beck, & Zhao, 2011) identified and described the most prevalent and valued types of academic writing from 12 high school classrooms in New York. Analytical writing, especially "exposition" was most prevalent on both high-stakes tests and in the classrooms (ESL and ELA) as well as most valued by the teachers. In particular, the three key features of exposition, such as the use of *source text, appropriate language conventions,* and *appropriate structure,* were considered most important for high school students. Interestingly, ESL teachers tended to prioritize *language conventions* and *mechanics* over any other elements, whereas none of the ELA teachers considered them the most important element in academic writing. In addition, "explanation," the analytical writing genre that appeared in the high-stakes ESL test, was not practiced or taught during any of the ESL classroom observations.

All the studies reviewed so far (except Llosa, Beck, & Zhao, 2011) did not necessarily focus on L2/multilingual adolescent students. They examined writing practices and instruction in middle and high school classrooms where both monolingual and multilingual students were taught. Yet, the findings certainly offer readers a general sense of types of writing activities and assignments for adolescent multilingual students in the classroom. The subsequent section discusses their writing experiences in content area classrooms.

Content Area Writing

Adolescent multilingual students likely spend most of their school time in the content area classrooms where writing plays a significant role in learning subject matters and demonstrating their learning. Yet, the role of content area writing has long been overlooked in the fields of L2 writing and L1 content area literacy (Enright & Gilliland, 2011; Kibler, 2011). This gap might be attributed to some prevalent perceptions, such as writing (literacy) instruction and content area learning are two different enterprises; English proficiency is a prerequisite for content area learning; or writing plays little or no role in learning in other content areas besides English language arts (Huang, 2004; Newell, 1998). Fortunately, a growing number of studies, although still very emerging, have examined multilingual students' writing in secondary content area classrooms (Bunch & Willett, 2013; Enright, 2013; Fránquiz & Salinas, 2011; Kibler, 2011; Wilcox & Jeffery, 2015). Here I focus on discussing some major findings from exemplary research on content area writing for adolescent multilingual students in English-medium educational contexts.

Challenges of Content Area Writing

As readers can imagine, content area writing is especially challenging for many multilingual writers. While learning English as an additional language, adolescent multilingual students need to develop academic writing, learn subject-matter materials, and demonstrate their content learning through writing. A real challenge of the development of content area writing can be attributed to the fact that there are various expectations for writing across content area classrooms. In other words, "the appropriate structure, register, and argumentation in these [academic] papers will vary across classes and disciplines" (Johns, 2008, p. 240). Adolescent multilingual students, thus, need to learn "content-specific strategies for understanding and creating texts according to discipline-specific norms and genres" (Enright, 2010, p. 805) and negotiate different writing tasks and demands across different content area classrooms.

Kibler's (2011) study examined possible sources of challenges adolescent multilingual students faced with content area writing tasks in the US high school. While comparing the perspectives of students and teachers with respect to the genre features and audience(s) for assigned writing tasks in Humanities and Biology classes, Kibler found a *difference* between ELs' and their content area teachers' perceptions of academic writing expectations. Apparently, implicit writing expectations existed for students in the content area classrooms (e.g., the Biology class teacher's notions of being "concise" and "write like a scientist" and the Humanities class teacher's notion of "clarity" in writing). Kibler suggested that teachers and students engage in more explicit discussions about disciplinary discourse norms, which can help ELs to become members of disciplinary discourse communities.

Similarly, several studies have also found some differences or dissonance between adolescent multilingual students and their teachers. For instance, Moje, Collazo, Carrillo, and Marx (2001) found a difference in how students and teachers interpreted writing assignments in a middle school inquiry-based science class. In addition, Ortmeier-Hooper's (2013) study revealed cultural dissonance between a refugee boy from Nigeria, called Wisdom, and his writing teacher in the English Language Arts classroom. Wisdom who identified himself as a writer was eager to learn and write in his ELA class, but the teacher did not understand Wisdom's refugee past and further called into question his academic dedication and attitude in class. Wisdom felt that he was misread by his writing teacher. Such experience of the dissonance between the two negatively influenced Wisdom's writing practice. For instance, Wisdom at one point "shut down," disengaging in the writing class. He "stopped 'putting his heart' in his writing" (p. 19). Collectively, the findings from these studies demonstrate that adolescent multilingual writers often experience some differences or gaps between them and their teachers in the content area classrooms, and such experiences tend to negatively influence their writing practices.

Exemplary Studies on Content Area Writing

Wilcox and her colleagues are leading scholars who have extensively examined content area writing for adolescent students (Graham, Early, & Wilcox, 2014; Wilcox, 2011; Wilcox & Jeffery, 2015; Wilcox, Yagelski, & Yu, 2014). In one of her earlier studies, Wilcox (2011) provided vivid descriptions of ways in which ELs engaged in writing across core content area classrooms (English, math, science, social studies) at the secondary level in a US public school setting. One of the intriguing findings was revealed from the comparison between ELs and non-EL students in these content area classrooms. In the social studies classrooms, English-speaking peers were asked to engage in analysis and syntheses of historical facts and concepts, whereas ELs engaged in simple mechanical writing activities, such as filling in the blanks and copying vocabulary and concepts in their packets, without much understanding of the meanings behind the texts. Similarly, in the science classrooms, Honors students were given more extended writing assignments for their portfolios, yet ELs' experiences and expectations of writing were quite different as reported by two 8th grade ELs, "We write [from] the overhead. When it's time for test, you study the notes and books and we play games" and "The only thing we do is write a lot of notes... a lot of notes and homework. For homework we look for the answer in the book [she shows a worksheet of fill in the blanks]" (p. 96). Overall, the teachers in all content areas required some writing, but "the expectations in terms of length, variety of uses, and cognitive dimensions in writing" (p. 99) were different for ELs as compared to native English-speaking peers. Furthermore, the teachers focused more on conventions of writing with ELs, whereas they encouraged English-speaking students to use writing as a means to express their ideas.

In another study, Wilcox and Jeffery (2015) focused on examining students' perspectives, or what they called "stance" toward content area writing. Stance here was defined as "'a display of a socially recognized point of view or attitude' (Ochs, 1993, p. 288), which includes students' expressions of how they feel about writing (affective stances) and what they know about writing (epistemic stances)" (Wilcox & Jeffery, 2015, p. 45). Overall, students tended to express more positive than negative stances toward school genres. When 26 participants were asked how they saw themselves as writers and of their experiences with writing, 17 out of 26 students expressed both positive (e.g., "I like to write") and negative affective stances (e.g., "I am not a big fan"). In addition, half of the students indicated a positive epistemic stance (e.g., "I actually think that I am a good writer"), and another half a negative epistemic stance (e.g., "I think it [my writing] is not really good") (p. 48). Notably, students seemed to see themselves as writers when they engaged with their preferred genres (i.e., diaries, adventure stories), but these genres were not used or taught in the classroom.

Bunch and Willett (2013) critically addressed another important topic in content area writing by investigating how adolescent multilingual students negotiate writing tasks and assignments in six middle-school social studies classrooms in the United States. In this research, the authors analyzed Reformation-unit essays by 40 students from six classrooms and found that the adolescent multilingual writers demonstrated their awareness of genre in various manners while taking advantage of their developing linguistic resources. For instance, some employed the features of expository essays (e.g., five-paragraph organization, topic sentences, transition words, third-person pronouns, and supporting details), and others used textual and rhetorical features of personal appeals (e.g., first- and second-person pronouns, emotional language, and vivid imagery or details to evoke audience's emotions). When they tried to represent their content knowledge, they drew on the curriculum and content encountered in the unit, explicitly referring to texts (oral, written, or visual) from curricular materials and additional outside texts to support their academic and personal arguments. Importantly, the students demonstrated content area learning "not merely by reproducing classroom texts, but by drawing from multiple resources to design their own texts to make sense of the curricular challenge the unit assignment posed" (p. 157).

Overall, it seems evident that adolescent multilingual students demonstrate their knowledge about the contents learned through their writing. Importantly, content area learning and writing development may be "interdependent" (Huang, 2004, p. 117) and mutually supportive, which suggests that researchers in the fields of content area learning and (L2) writing pay more attention to the *intersection* of the two.

In the subsequent sections, I discuss some of the most salient topics and lines of inquiry in adolescent multilingual writing research, such as (a) writing processes, strategies, and products, (b) linguistic factors influencing academic writing (e.g., L1 and L2 proficiency), (c) identity construction, and (d) the use of technology. Although there are some other important issues in adolescent multilingual writing, these topics seem to be most pertinent to academic writing experiences and expectations for adolescent multilingual writers.

Writing Processes, Strategies, and Products

Writing processes, strategies, and products are always inextricably linked and part of ongoing meaning-making. This section focuses on discussing writing processes, strategies, and products, which helps researchers and practitioners understand writing development of adolescent multilingual students. A writing process has been one of the most frequently discussed topics in L2 writing research. Since Emig's (1971) research of English-speaking high school students' composing processes, the process writing approach has been one of the most widely adapted writing approaches in the classroom. In the US context, it was validated when the National Council of Teachers of English (NCTE) and the International Reading Association (IRA) jointly published Content Standard 5 for the English Language Arts, K-12: "Students employ a wide range of *strategies* as they write and use different *writing process* elements appropriately to communicate with different audiences for a variety of purposes" (NCTE, 1996) (emphasis added). Thus, the process approach to teaching writing appears to have been "gold standard" for instruction in K-12 classrooms (Pritchard & Honeycutt, 2006, p. 277).

L2 writing researchers have examined writing processes, especially in relation to how L2/multilingual writers use strategies of planning, drafting, and revising. While they have argued that there is no agreed definition of "process" that accounts for all L2/multilingual writers, research has focused on the multiplicity of processes underlying various writers (both successful and unsuccessful) have. Hedgcock (2012, p. 231) synthesizes L2 writing process research and summarizes salient findings about writing processes of *successful L2 writers*. They tend to do the following:

* plan their writing more extensively and elaboratively,
* evaluate and rework their plans more frequently,
* strategically and mindfully pursue a wider range of solutions to rhetorical problems,
* envision reader expectations as they plan and revise, accommodating multiple viewpoints in their texts,

- revise globally, avoiding the temptation to overedit locally,
- deploy more (and more effective) planning, drafting, and revision strategies.

Although Hedgcock's synthesis above provides researchers and practitioners with important insights into writing processes of successful L2 writers, it was conducted based on the research on college and adult L2 writers who tend to have L1 writing skills and knowledge to varying degrees. It has been almost a decade since Hedgcock's synthesis was published, yet the lack of research on adolescent multilingual students' writing processes still remains. Below I report and discuss some major findings from a few empirical studies on writing processes, strategies, and products of adolescent multilingual writers in English-medium instructional contexts.

Exemplary Studies on Writing Processes, Strategies, and Products

The first study I would like to introduce is an ethnographic study on how Quebec Francophone high school students *appropriated* the writing process over the course of 4 years (grades 7–10) in their ESL Language Arts classes in Canada (Parks, Huot, Hamers, & Lemonnier, 2005). The participating students were first introduced the writing process in grade 7 by their ESL Language Arts teacher who favored the use of the writing process. By grade 10, they were very familiar with multiple steps of writing and were able to readily describe them. The students engaged in a self-regulated process (e.g., students enacted their own writing processes) and an other-regulated process (e.g., being told by teacher about when and how to proceed). In addition, some students had begun to transfer the use of writing process from an ESL classroom to other writing contexts; others took a more flexible approach to the writing process by adapting it. For instance, some students came to learn that a certain teacher paid attention to final products only, and such teacher's action influenced students' writing process (paying less attention to the process like brainstorming). Furthermore, students with more autonomous use of the writing process "had come to value the writing process as a tool (i.e., resource/strategy) which could be used to this end" (p. 252). Overall, the adolescent multilingual students negotiated their own writing processes as they developed their academic writing.

Another study by Danzak (2011b) is unique in that it examined bilingual writing, not just English writing, of 20 Spanish-speaking ELs in an American middle school. She analyzed two expository and two narrative autobiographic texts, each in both English and Spanish, using quantitative tools. The study examined if there was any evidence of language transfer (between English and Spanish) in the students' bilingual writing and how genre (expository and narrative) influenced products at the lexical, syntactic, and discourse levels. One of the important findings was that significant differences in lexical, syntactic, and discourse levels were generally based more on the topic of the writing prompt rather than the genre, which suggests the importance of selecting meaningful topics to engage adolescent multilingual writers. In addition, the study found some evidence of language transfer in a bidirectional manner that "knowledge and application of general academic writing skills appeared to traverse linguistic boundaries" across English and Spanish (Danzak, 2011b, p. 501). In terms of writing strategies use, these emergent bilingual writers tended to employ a "knowledge-telling strategy" (Bereiter & Scardamalia, 1987, p. 5) through which they took some cues from the writing prompt and produced a text by simply writing down everything they could recall about the given topic (Danzak, 2011b, p. 501). Overall, this study contributed to deepening our understanding of the nature of bilingual writing for adolescent emergent bilinguals.

In a more recent study, Smith, Pacheco, & de Almeida (2017) examined three bilingual students' processes of composing across languages (L1, L2) and non-linguistic modes (e.g., images and sounds) in an 8th grade English class at an urban school in the United States. Unlike much of previous writing process research, this research uniquely focused on the writing processes across languages and non-linguistics modes. The researchers called this process "multimodal codemeshing" (p. 6). Three participants orchestrated various modes and media (including written words in English and their heritage language, images, voice recordings, background music, and slide animations) to create their "My Hero" projects, that is, a multimodal presentation on his or her personal hero. At first, students engaged in their multimodal codemeshing process by becoming familiarized with various features of the composing tool (e.g., editing sounds, searching online for open access material), collaborating with peers, and visually brainstorming while gathering information and organizing the structure of their presentations. After this phase, the students skillfully navigated multiple modes, purposefully switched between English and their heritage language, and iteratively moved across different parts of their PowerPoint presentations to construct meaningful content. For instance, when a Vietnamese-English bilingual student worked on one slide for her PowerPoint presentation, she constantly traversed across image searching (using both English and Vietnamese), image editing, and writing for that slide about 11 times for 22 minutes. Overall, the participants displayed both "textually-driven and visually-driven processes" (p. 6) to create multimodal texts. The findings of this research seem to contribute to broadening the notion of writing (processes) by considering multiple languages (not just English only) and non-linguistic semiotic resources (images and sounds).

Finally, Wilcox and her colleagues' study about writing products (Wilcox, Yagelski, & Yu, 2014) is worth noting here. They examined the nature and frequency of *errors in writing* by high school students, both ELs and non-ELs, while comparing their writing samples from their ELA and social studies classes. The writing samples were from the larger study, called the National Study of Writing Instruction in which Applebee and Langer (2009, 2011, 2013) examined the nature of writing instruction across disciplines in ten high schools in 5 states in the United States. For this writing error study, Wilcox and her colleagues analyzed 178 essays (120 in ELA and 58 in social studies) from 67 students (33 10th graders and 34 12th graders; 18 ELs and 49 non-ELs). One of the important findings was that adolescent students' errors did not necessarily reflect a "crisis in writing ability" nor support the common concern that "adolescent students lack basic skills in written English" (p. 1085). For instance, the most common errors were not serious syntactical errors that could potentially interfere with comprehension, but rather minor errors, such as spelling error, incorrect verb inflection, capitalization error, and missing words. These were the top four errors for both ELs and non-ELs in this order, showing there was no significant difference in error types made by ELs and non-ELs. Yet, ELs' error rate was higher than non-ELs', which is not surprising.

Collectively, these exemplary studies give researchers and practitioners valuable insights into the writing processes, strategies, and products, which further helps understand the complex nature of writing development of adolescent multilingual students. The subsequent section focuses on discussing linguistic factors that influence academic writing development.

L1 and L2 Proficiency Influencing Academic Writing

Among many factors influencing L2 academic writing, L1 (oral language), L2 reading, and L2 proficiency are those that are most significant. Recent studies, especially those from a sociocultural perspective, have found that L1 plays an important mediating role in learning and developing L2 writing. Although the majority of studies on the L1 use in L2 writing have been conducted in college classrooms, there are several notable studies that specifically addressed adolescent multilingual writers' L1 use. For instance, Kibler (2010) and de la Piedra (2010) found that their Spanish-English bilingual adolescents took advantage of their L1 while producing L2 texts. Kibler's (2010) study focused on the L1 use among peers around L2 writing tasks in a content area classroom. In this study, focal participants were four Latino adolescents of upper beginning to intermediate English proficiency levels in a grade 10 Humanities class. The focal writing task was part of the student work for the unit of Industrialization. After reading an Industrialization-related novel, the students assumed one character's viewpoint and wrote a letter to another character, expressing their opinions on (dis)advantages about Industrialization based on their life experiences. Spanish as their L1 was used among students to "share difficulties, ask questions, and help each other generate ideas" (p. 122). All four participants, mostly during peer interactions, demonstrated expertise in at least one aspect of knowledge (e.g., knowledge of task, content, rhetorical form, and linguistic form) through L1 use. Although this research did not necessarily evaluate the use of L1 for the improvement of L2 writing, the use of L1, especially their oral interactions in Spanish (L1), helped adolescent ELs manage academically and cognitively challenging writing tasks and position themselves as experts, not just deficit limited English proficient students, in certain aspects of writing in the content area classroom.

Similarly, Spanish-English speaking transnational middle school students in de la Piedra's (2010) study produced collaborative texts (scripts, narratives, posters, and presentations), using both Spanish and English. In preparing a class presentation, they read the information written in Spanish, spoke Spanish to explain the meanings from the texts, and brainstormed and drafted in Spanish, although the final products were English-dominant bilingual texts. Adolescent multilingual students in both studies (de la Piedra, 2010; Kibler, 2010) used Spanish to better make sense of text and produce more coherent texts. Their L1 was "a productive affordance" for multilingual students when they completed L2 writing tasks in the classroom (Kibler, 2010, p. 122). Further research is needed on under what contexts or conditions the use of L1 could be effective in L2 writing.

In addition to a first language, L2 reading and L2 proficiency are other significant factors influencing L2 academic writing. Numerous studies have found possible interconnections among L2 writing, L2 reading, and L2 proficiency. For instance, Lee (2005) examined how five factors (i.e., free reading, free writing, writing apprehension, writer's block, and students' attitude toward reading/writing instruction) interacted with one another and found free (voluntary) reading in L2 was the only significant facilitative predictor of L2 writing performance for Taiwanese college students. Similarly, Ito (2011) found from Japanese EFL high school students that their reading skills in L2 partly influenced the quality of their L2 writing.

A more recent study by Lee and Schallert (2016) found *mutual influence* of reading and writing in L2, that is, the facilitative effect between reading and writing in L2 was bi-directional for 300 Korean EFL middle school students. This research revealed that a certain level (threshold) of L2 proficiency (the two highest levels – 4 and 5 – in this study) was required to achieve significant gains in writing scores, although most students (all but level 1 L2 proficiency) improved in their reading comprehension. Interestingly, students at levels 2 and 3 showed the improvement in reading but *not writing*. In other words, the reading-writing connections seemed to be evident for students who achieved a certain level of L2 proficiency (levels 4 and 5). Here we can see the influence of L2 proficiency on growth in academic writing in L2. In fact, Pae's (2018) study also revealed a similar finding that L2 proficiency significantly moderated the relationship between L1 and L2 writing skills, but it did not for the relationship between L1 and L2 reading skills. All these studies were conducted in EFL contexts, and thus the findings could be different for ESL contexts, but these findings teach us that there could be potential interactions among L2 proficiency, L2 reading, and L2 writing, while L2 reading and L2 proficiency are likely to influence L2 academic writing.

Identity and Academic Writing

Identity is one of the most frequently discussed topics in adolescent writing and literacy. Here I like to discuss how identity is influenced by and influences academic writing practices. A growing number of L2 writing scholars have found that many adolescent multilingual students engage in exploring and expressing identities through writing practices in the classroom (de Oliveira & Silva, 2003; Harklau & Moreno, 2019; Ortmeier-Hooper & Enright, 2011; Yi, 2013). Their academic writing practices can play a significant role as "identity enhancement" (McKay & Wong 1996, p. 603). In addition, in terms of identity-theory building, explorations into multilingual writers' identity and literacy practices are especially compelling because such findings from multilingual writers, who tend to travel multiple languages, literacies, and identities, enable literacy scholars to better "conceptualize identities in multiple and contradictory ways" (Yi, 2010, p. 304).

Some L2 writing studies examined the relationship between identity construction and academic writing by implementing identity-oriented instructional units (e.g., Lopez & Musanti, 2019; Wilson, Chavez, & Anders, 2012) or writing tasks through which students were asked to express and represent their identities (Danzak, 2011a). For instance, Wilson, Chavez, and Anders (2012) examined how adolescent ELs used multiple forms of representation to express an identity they valued while implementing an 18-week unit on "identity" into the 8th grade English Language Development class in the United States. One of the unit objectives was to use writing to reflect their own identities. Eight intermediate ELs in the class engaged in various sophisticated literacy activities, such as making a character web for the book they read, composed "I Am From" poems, interviewed family members about their heritage, wrote about significant life events, and finally created a digital podcast (digital compilations of audio and visual files) through which the participants expressed some important aspects of their selves. These academic literacy practices allowed them to instantiate *distinctive identities* in their podcasts, emphasizing different aspects of their lives (e.g., family members, items they liked, popular culture, and life events) as being salient to them to varying degrees.

In some studies, adolescent multilingual students were asked to produce "identity texts" defined as "artifacts that students produce whereby they take ownership of their learning" (Fránquiz & Salinas, 2011, p. 200). For instance, newcomer students in an American high school were asked to author identity texts, that is a collage in which they labeled pictures with academic concepts in both Spanish and English (e.g., discriminación and discrimination), wrote letters to Latina/o Civil Rights Organizations, and responded to questions about present-day immigration marches (Fránquiz & Salinas, 2011). When the high school newcomers responded to writing prompts, they especially positioned themselves in the shoes of historical individuals and tended to produce identity texts. The acceptance of using both languages, digitized documents, and relevant genres (letters) elicited "identity investment in the production of writing" (p. 196).

In a slightly different, semi-academic, after-school context, the power of authoring identity texts was also manifested. Daniel (2019) designed, implemented, and examined an afterschool writing workshop, called "Writing Our Identities for Successful Endeavors

(WISE)" in her designed-based research. In this writing workshop, refugee youth in the United States discussed their futures (e.g., career aspirations, personalized goals) as well as analyzed and wrote identity texts to prepare for writing college application essays and interviewing for jobs. Creating and talking about their identity texts afforded them opportunities to develop multilingual literacy skills, increase their sense of self, and demonstrate their high aspirations about their future. In addition, their identity texts and discussions about them show "how ambitious they are, how much they hope to contribute to their communities, and how they view themselves as having rich potential to make significant, positive impacts in the world" (p. 80), which challenges deficit discourses about refugee teens.

Some studies specifically documented a *writerly identity* negotiated through writing practices in the classroom (Hughes & Morrison, 2014; Lopez & Musanti, 2019; Ortmeier-Hooper, 2013; Skerrett, 2013). For instance, 6th grade ELs in a Canadian public school (Hughes & Morrison, 2014) developed writerly identities while learning about five genres of poetry that related to identity and identity construction. The students wrote an acrostic poem using their names, made a personal "About Me" poster, created their online postcard poems, responding to the prompt, "Who I want to be in middle school," created a poem using iMovie, and responded to "Who I Am?" Overall, students' writing experiences and practices helped them (1) feel more comfortable writing in English and (2) construct positive writerly identities.

All the studies described thus far have looked into how adolescent multilingual students use writing to reflect who they are and to negotiate their identities. Conversely, students' identities also can influence their writing practices as well, which has been relatively less discussed in L2 writing research. For instance, Hoon, a Korean-speaking high school boy, experienced a stigma attached to his ESL service and learning, and thus he deliberately tried to develop an academic achiever identity so as to resist his stigmatized ESL-student identity (Yi, 2013). Unfortunately, in the process of such negotiation of multiple identities (a stigmatized ESL identity and an academic achiever identity), Hoon developed his own survival strategies that helped him earn high grades but prevented him from engaging in extensive academic writing activities. For instance, he avoided taking courses that required extensive academic writing activities and assignments. Instead, he deliberately selected elective courses (e.g., "Global Gourmet," "Introduction to Technology," "Computer Graphic and New Media," and "Drawing") where writing was minimally required, and so he could receive high grades. This particular survival strategy served him well to gain high grades and construct an academic achiever identity, yet he lost opportunities to practice and develop academic writing.

I have so far discussed how adolescent multilingual students use writing to negotiate, perform, and project their identities as well as how their identities influence their writing practices for school. Now, I would like to move on to another most salient issue in adolescent multilingual writing research, which is the role and use of technology. These two issues of identity construction and use of technology complicate the nature of adolescent multilingual writing for school.

Technology and Academic Writing

Much of the writing in contemporary schools and workplaces uses digital and multimedia tools. Students are raised in a digital world where they use technology in every aspect of their daily lives. A few recent reviews on technology and academic writing (Galvin & Greenhow, 2020; Williams & Beam, 2019) collectively pointed out that very little research has been done with and for adolescent multilingual writers. I, however, need to acknowledge that there is a lag between classroom practices reported in published research and actual practices in the current classroom. I believe more teachers are integrating different types of technology into the classroom. Among various kinds of writing with emerging technologies, this section focuses on discussing *digital multimodal writing* practice in the classroom given its prominence in the classroom and literacy research (Belcher, 2017).

Digital Multimodal Writing: Affordances and Possibilities for Academic Writing

Teachers have engaged their adolescent multilingual students into a wide range of digital multimodal writing, such as "digital storytelling" (Anderson, Chung, & Maclerory, 2018; Honeyford, 2013; Vu, Warschaure, & Yim, 2019); "blogging" (Reinhardt, 2019), making "PowerPoint slides" (Shin, 2018; Smith et al., 2017), and managing "social networking sites" (Andrei, 2019; Vanek, King, & Bigelow, 2018), among others. These digital multimodal writing practices afford adolescent multilingual writers to improve L2 writing and L2 proficiency, make connections with their home language and culture, explore and express identities, deepen content area learning, and increase creativity and critical perspectives (see reviews of research on digital multimodal writing for multilingual students in Smith, Pacheco, and Khorosheva in 2021 and Yi, Shin, and Cimasko in 2019).

Digital multimodal writing practices help adolescent multilingual students develop their L2 academic writing and L2 proficiency by offering them more meaningful and authentic writing opportunities, allowing them to experience diverse types of texts, helping expand their views of writing, and increasing motivation for and engagement with writing (Danzak, 2011b; Hepple, Sockhill, Tan, & Alford, 2014; Shin, Cimasko, & Yi, 2020; Smith et al., 2017). For instance, adolescent ELs with *low* English literacy in Australia (Hepple, Sockhill, Tan, & Alford, 2014) engaged in "claymations" (clay animation, that is one of forms of stop-motion animation) projects through which the students experimented with various ways of expressing ideas, understood and developed narratives, and experienced a variety of collaborative and authentic writing opportunities (e.g., analyzing texts; creating a storyboard and models; writing scenarios, captions, and dialogues; and filming and narrating a story); 6th grade bilingual students in the United States developed metalinguistic awareness and metalanguage, which is vital to developing academic language, through digital multimodal narrative and argumentative writing (e.g., making PowerPoint slides and online posters) (Shin, Cimasko, & Yi, 2020). Furthermore, 8th grade bilingual students in the United States (Smith et al., 2017) engaged in a "My Hero" digital multimodal project (a PowerPoint presentation) through which they experienced authentic writing and diverse genres; skillfully traversed text, images, and sound; and coordinated them for different communicative affordances, indicating that they likely developed "multimodal communicative competence" (Royce, 2002, p. 191).

Second, much of the research on adolescent multilingual students' digital multimodal writing has shown that they connected with their home land and culture and performed their identities through such writing practices. By infusing some aspects of their identities to their digital multimodal writing, adolescent multilingual students showcased their heritage language and culture (Honeyford, 2014; Noguerón-Liu & Hogan, 2017). In addition, as extensively discussed in the previous section on identity and academic writing, adolescent ELs used digital multimodal writing to express their multiple identities (Hughes & Morrison, 2014; Wilson, Chavez, & Anders, 2012).

Third, digital multimodal writing helps promote content area learning. When digital multimodal writing is integrated into classroom practices, students are asked to work toward academic learning goals through digital multimodal writing. In addition, there are some significant aspects of digital multimodal writing that are conducive to content learning (Yi, Shin, & Cimasko, 2019), such as collaborative learning opportunities in digital multimodal writing practices (e.g., Cummins, Hu, Markus, & Montero, 2015; Hepple et al., 2014). In Burke and Hardware's (2015) study, immigrant students in an urban grade 8 Canadian classroom deepened their understanding of a novel with themes centered around life and death (e.g., comprehending from various participant perspectives around themes) while engaging in their digital photostory project. Digital multimodal writing projects enhanced the learning opportunities for these students in a Language Arts class, which has similarly been reported in other studies wherein adolescent multilingual students conducted the analysis and interpretation of literature through digital multimodal writing projects (Ajayi, 2015; Smith et al., 2017).

Finally, digital multimodal writing helps students increase critical language and literacy awareness (Ajayi, 2015; Walsh, 2009) and foster creativity (Anderson, Chung, & Maclerory, 2018; Choi & Yi, 2016). Ajayi is a leading scholar who has examined multilingual students' digital multimodal literacy practices from a critical perspective. One of his latest works (Ajayi, 2015) found that three female Nigerian high school students critiqued the messages of social inequality in the textbook they read, questioned the social production of gender in Nigeria, made personal connections, and created an agentive self through multimodal writing practices. In addition, the findings suggest that critical multimodal literacy practices "may become increasingly central to understanding how students develop a critical analysis of texts, subvert gender relations, and feel empowered to critique unequal social structures" (p. 239).

Concluding Remarks about Adolescent Multilingual Writing in School

Surveying research on adolescent multilingual students and their writing for academic purposes seems to teach researchers two areas that are needed to further investigate in the future. Although there are many longitudinal qualitative studies on academic writing, researchers still do not seem to know enough about how bi- and multilingual students develop home language and literacy, along with academic English and writing over longer stretches of time. As Graham (2019) rightfully states, "writing develops across the life span, some forms of writing take many years to master, and writing growth is a consequence of writing and deliberate practice" (p. 286). As such, writing grows and changes over time, so does bi- and multilingual writing. Given that, tracing students' "writing across lifespan" (Bazerman, 2016 – Dartmouth Institute and Conference), while extremely challenging, may help researchers and practitioners learn more about how people learn to write in more than one language, how writing in multiple languages develops over time, and what role writing plays in life. In addition, I have found various purposes or functions of academic writing (e.g., writing to communicate, learn, explore identities, and position themselves) from existing literature, yet little research seems to address writing for civic engagement or social action in the multilingual contexts. I would like to invite researchers and educators to explore writing for social change and action.

References

Ajayi, L. (2015). Critical multimodal literacy: How Nigerian female students critique texts and reconstruct unequal social structures. *Journal of Literacy Research, 47*(2), 216–244. https://doi.org/10.1177/1086296X15618478

Anderson, J., Chung, Y., & Maclerory, V. (2018). Creative and critical approaches to language learning and digital technology: Findings from a multilingual digital storytelling project. *Language & Education, 32*(3), 195–211. https://doi.org/10.1080/09500782.2018.1430151

Andrei, E. (2019). Adolescent English learners' use of digital technology in the classroom. *The Educational Forum, 83*(1), 102–120. https://doi.org/10.1080/00131725.2018.1478474

Anstrom, K., DiCerbo, P., Butler, F., Katz, A., Millet, J., & Rivera, C. (2010). *A review of the literature on academic English: Implications for K-12 English language learners.* Arlington, VA: The George Washington University Center for Equity and Excellence in Education.

Applebee, A. N., & Langer, J. A. (2009). What is happening in the teaching of writing? *English Journal, 98*(5), 18–28.

Applebee, A. N., & Langer, J. A. (2011). A snapshot of writing instruction in middle schools and high schools. *English Journal, 100*(6), 14–27.

Applebee, A. N., & Langer, J. A. (2013). *Writing instruction that works: Proven methods for middle and high school classrooms.* New York: Teachers College.

Bazerman, C. (2016). *The puzzle of conducting research on lifespan development of writing abilities.* 50th Anniversary Dartmouth Institute and Conference.

Belcher, D. (2017). On becoming facilitators of multimodal composing and digital design. *Journal of Second Language Writing, 38*, 80–85. http://dx.doi.org/10.1016/j.jslw.2017.10.004

Bereiter, C., & Scardamalia, M. (Eds.) (1987). *The psychology of written composition.* Hillsdale, NJ: Erlbaum. https://doi.org/10.4324/9780203812310

Bunch, G. (2006). "Academic English" in the 7th grade: Broadening the lens, expanding access. *Journal of English for Academic Purposes, 5*(4), 284–301. https://doi.org/10.1016/j.jeap.2006.08.007

Bunch, G., & Willett, K. (2013). Writing to mean in middle school: Understanding how second language writers negotiate textually-rich content-area instruction. *Journal of Second Language Writing, 22*(2), 141–160. https://doi.org/10.1016/j.jslw.2013.03.007

Burke, A., & Hardware, S. (2015). Honouring ESL students' lived experiences in school learning with multiliteracies pedagogy. *Language, Culture, & Curriculum, 28*(2), 143–157. https://doi.org/10.1080/07908318.2015.1027214

Chamot, A. U., & O'Malley, J. M. (1994). *The CALLA handbook: Implementing the cognitive academic language learning approach.* New York: Longman.

Choi, J., & Yi, Y. (2016). Teachers' integration of multimodal into classroom practices for English language learners. *TESOL Journal, 7*(2), 304–327. https://doi.org/10.1002/tesj.204

Cummins, J., Hu, S., Markus, P., & Montero, M. K. (2015). Identity texts and academic achievement: Connecting the dots in multilingual school contexts. *TESOL Quarterly, 49*(3), 555–581. https://doi.org/10.1002/tesq.241

Daniel, S. (2019). Writing our identities for successful endeavors: Resettled refugee youth look to the future. *Journal of Research in Childhood Education, 33*(1), 71–83. https://doi.org/10.1080/02568543.2018.1531448

Danzak, R. L. (2011a). Defining identities through multiliteracies: EL teens narrate their immigration experiences as graphic stories. *Journal of Adolescent & Adult Literacy, 55*(3), 187–196. https://doi.org/10.1002/JAAL.00024

Danzak, R. L. (2011b). The integration of lexical, syntactic, and discourse features in bilingual adolescents' writing: An exploratory approach. *Language, Speech, and Hearing Services in Schools, 42*(4), 491–505. https://doi.org/10.1044/0161-1461(2011/10-0063)

de la Piedra, M. T. (2010). Adolescent worlds and literacy practices on the United States- Mexico border. *Journal of Adolescent & Adult Literacy, 53*(7), 575–584. https://doi.org/10.1598/JAAL.53.7.5

de Oliveira, L. C., & Silva, T. (Eds.). (2013). *L2 writing in secondary classrooms: Student experiences, academic issues, and teacher education.* New York: Routledge.

Emig, J. (1971). *The composing processes of twelfth graders.* Urbana, IL: National Council of Teachers of English.

Enright, K. A. (2010). Academic literacies and adolescent learners: English for subject-matter secondary classrooms. *TESOL Quarterly, 44*(4), 804–810. https://doi: 10.5054/tq.2010.237336

Enright, K. A. (2013). Adolescent writers and academic trajectories: Situating L2 writing in the content areas. In L.C. de Oliveira & T. Silva (Eds.), *L2 Writing in the Secondary Classroom: Experiences, Issues, and Teacher Education* (pp. 27–43) New York: Routledge. https://doi.org/10.4324/9780203082669

Enright, K. A., & Gilliland, B. (2011). Multilingual writing in an age of accountability: From policy to practice in U.S. high school classrooms. *Journal of Second Language Writing, 20*(3), 182–195. https://doi.org/10.1016/j.jslw.2011.05.006

Fillmore, L. W., & Snow, C. (2000). *What teachers need to know about language.* Clearinghouse on Language and Linguistics Special Report. https://people.ucsc.edu/~ktellez/wong-fill-snow.html

82   *Multilingual Writing in School*

Fránquiz, M., & Salinas, C. (2011). Newcomers developing English literacy through historical thinking and digitized primary sources. *Journal of Second Language Writing, 20*(3), 196–210. https://doi.org/10.1016/j.jslw.2011.05.004

Galvin, S., & Greenhow, C. (2020). Writing on social media: A review of research in the high school classroom. *TechTrends, 64,* 57–69. https://doi.org/10.1007/s11528-019-00428-9

Gentil, G. (2011). A biliteracy agenda for genre research. *Journal of Second Language Writing, 20*(1), 6–23. https://doi.org/10.1016/j.jslw.2010.12.006

Graham, S. (2019). Changing how writing is taught. *Review of Research in Education, 43*(1), 277–303. https://doi.org/10.3102/0091732X18821125

Graham, S., Capizzi, A., Harris, K. R., Hebert, M., & Morphy, P. (2014). Teaching writing to middle school students: a national survey. *Reading & Writing, 27,* 1015–1042. https://doi.org/10.1007/s11145-013-9495-7

Graham, S., Early, J., & Wilcox, K. (2014). Adolescent writing and writing instruction: Introduction to the special issue. *Reading & Writing, 27*(6), 969–972.

Haneda, M. (2014). From academic language to academic communication: Building on English learners' resources. *Linguistics and Education, 26,* 126–135. https://doi.org/10.1016/j.linged.2014.01.004

Harklau, L., & Moreno, R. (2019). The adolescent English language learner: Identities lost and found. In X. Gao (Ed.), *Second handbook of English language teaching* (pp. 601–620). New York: Springer. https://doi.org/10.1007/978-3-030-02899-2

Hedgcock, J. S. (2012). Second language writing processes among adolescent and adult learners. In E. L. Grigorenko, E. Mambrino & D. D. Preiss (Eds.), *Writing: A mosaic of new perspectives* (pp. 221–239). New York: Psychology Press.

Hepple, E., Sockhill, M., Tan, A., & Alford, J. (2014). Multiliteracies pedagogy: Creating claymations with adolescent, post-beginner English language learners. *Journal of Adolescent & Adult Literacy, 58*(3), 219–229. https://doi.org/10.1002/jaal.339

Honeyford, M. (2014). From *Aquí* and *Allá*: Symbolic convergence in the multimodal literacy practices of adolescent immigrant students. *Journal of Literacy Research, 46*(2), 194–233. https://doi.org/10.1177%2F1086296X14534180

Huang, J. (2004). Socialising ESL students into the discourse of school science through academic writing. *Language & Education, 18*(2), 97–123. https://doi.org/10.1080/09500780408666870

Hughes, J. M., & Morrison, L. (2014). The impact of social networking and a multiliteracies pedagogy on English language learners' writer identities. *Writing & Pedagogy, 6*(3), 607–631. https://doi.org/10.1558/wap.v6i3.607

Ito, F. (2011). L2 reading–writing correlation in Japanese EFL high school students. *The Language Teacher, 35*(5), 23–29. https://doi.org/10.37546/JALTTLT35.5-2

Johns, A. (2008). Genre awareness for the novice academic student: An ongoing quest. *Language Teaching, 41*(2), 237–252. doi:10.1017/S0261444807004892 https://ila.onlinelibrary.wiley.com/doi/abs/10.1002/jaal.719

Kibler, A. (2010). Writing through two languages: First language expertise in a language minority classroom. *Journal of Second Language Writing, 19*(3), 121–142. https://doi.org/10.1016/j.jslw.2010.04.001

Kibler, A. (2011). "I write in a way that people can read it": How teachers and adolescent L2 writers describe content area writing. *Journal of Second Language Writing, 20*(3), 211–226. https://doi.org/10.1016/j.jslw.2011.05.005

Kibler, A. (2014). From high school to the *noviciado*: An adolescent linguistic minority student's multilingual journey in writing. *The Modern Language Journal, 98*(2), 629–651. https://doi.org/10.1111/modl.12090

Kiuhara, S. A., Graham, S., & Hawken, L. S. (2009). Teaching writing to high school students: A national survey. *Journal of Educational Psychology, 101*, 136–160. https://psycnet.apa.org/doi/10.1037/a0013097

Lawrence, J. F., Galloway. E. P., Yim, S., & Lin, A. (2013). Learning to write in middle school? Insights into adolescent writers' instructional experiences across content areas. *Journal of Adolescent & Adult Literacy, 57*(2), 151–161. https://doi.org/10.1002/JAAL.219

Lea, M., & Street, B. (2006). The "academic literacies" model: Theory and applications. *Theory into Practice, 45*(4), 368–377. https://doi.org/10.1207/s15430421tip4504_11

Lee, J., & Schallert, D. L. (2016). Exploring the reading-writing connection: A yearlong classroom-based experimental study of middle school students developing literacy in a new language. *Reading Research Quarterly, 51*(2), 143–164. https://doi.org/10.1002/rrq.132

Lee, S. (2005). Facilitating and inhibiting factors in English as a foreign language writing performance: A model testing with structural equation modeling. *Language Learning: A Journal of Research in Language Studies, 55*(2), 335–374. https://doi.org/10.1111/j.0023-8333.2005.00306.x

Llosa, L., Beck, S. W., & Zhao, C. G. (2011). An investigation of academic writing in secondary schools to inform the development of diagnostic classroom assessments. *Assessing Writing, 16*(4), 256–73. https://doi.org/10.1016/j.asw.2011.07.001

Lopez, C. G., & Musanti, S. I. (2019). Fostering identity negotiation in sixth-grade ELLS: Examining an instructional unit on identity in English Language Arts. *NABE Journal of Research and Practice, 9*(2), 61–77. https://doi.org/10.1080/26390043.2019.1589290

McKay, S. L., & Wong, S. C. (1996). Multiple discourses, multiple identities: Investment and agency in second language learning among Chinese adolescent immigrant students. *Harvard Educational Review, 66*(3), 577–609. https://doi.org/10.17763/haer.66.3.n47r06u264944865

Moje, E. B., Collazo, T., Carrillo, R., & Marx, R. W. (2001). "Maestro, what is 'quality'?": Language, literacy, and discourse in project-based science. *Journal of Research in Science Teaching, 38*(4), 469–498. https://doi.org/10.1002/tea.1014

Molle, D., Sato, E., Boals, T., & Hedgspeth, C. A. (Eds.). (2015). *Multilingual learners and academic literacies: Sociocultural contexts of literacy development in adolescents*. New York: Routledge.

84   *Multilingual Writing in School*

National Commission on Writing in America's Schools and Colleges (2003). *The Neglected "R": The Need for a Writing Revolution.* New York: The College Board.

Newell, G. E. (1998). 'How much are we the wiser?': Continuity and change in writing and learning in the content areas. In N. Nelson & R. C. Calfee (Eds.), *The reading-writing connection, ninety-seventh yearbook of the national society for the study of education, Part II* (pp. 178–202). Chicago IL: University of Chicago Press.

Noguerón-Liu, S., & Hogan, J. J. (2017). Remembering Michoacán: Digital representations of the homeland by immigrant adults and adolescents. *Research in the Teaching of English, 51*(3), 267–289.

Ochs, E. (1993). Constructing social identity: A language socialization perspective. *Research on language and Social Interaction, 26*(3), 287–306. https://doi.org/10.1207/s15327973rlsi2603_3

Ortmeier-Hooper, C. (2013). "She doesn't know who I am": The case of a refugee L2 writer in a high school English language arts classroom. In L. C. de Oliveira & T. Silva (Eds.) *L2 writing in secondary classrooms: Student experiences, academic issues, and teacher education* (pp. 9–26). New York: Routledge.

Ortmeier-Hooper, C., & Enright, K. A. (2011). Mapping new territory: Toward an understanding of adolescent L2 writers and writing in US contexts. *Journal of Second Language Writing, 20*(3), 167–181. https://doi.org/10.1016/j.jslw.2011.05.002

Pacheco, M. (2015). Bilingualism-as-participation: Examining adolescents' bi(multi)lingual literacies across out-of-school and online contexts. In D. Molle, E. Sato, T. Boals & C. A. Hedgspeth (Eds.), *Multilingual learners and academic literacies: Sociocultural contexts of literacy development* (pp. 135–165). New York: Routledge.

Pae, T. (2018). A simultaneous analysis of relations between L1 and L2 skills in reading and writing. *Reading Research Quarterly, 54*(1), 109–124. https://doi.org/10.1002/rrq.216

Parks, S., Huot, D., Hamers, J., & Lemonnier, F. (2005). "History of theatre" web sites: A brief history of the writing process in a high school ESL language arts class. *Journal of Second Language Writing, 14*(4), 233–258. https://doi.org/10.1016/j.jslw.2005.10.003

Pritchard, R. J., & Honeycutt, R. L. (2006). The process approach to writing instruction: Examining its effectiveness. In C. A. MacArthur, S. Graham & J. Fitzgerald (Eds.), *Handbook of writing research* (pp. 275–290). New York: Guilford Press.

Reinhardt, J. (2019). Social media in second and foreign language teaching and learning: Blogs, wikis, and social networking. *Language Teaching, 52*(1), 1–39. https://doi.org/10.1017/S0261444818000356

Royce, T. (2002). Multimodality in the TESOL classroom: Exploring visual-verbal synergy. *TESOL Quarterly, 36*(2). 191–205. https://doi.org/10.2307/3588330

Scarcella, R. (2003). *Academic English: A conceptual framework.* The University of California Linguistic Minority Research Institute. https://escholarship.org/uc/item/6pd082d4

Schleppegrell, M. J. (2012). Academic language in teaching and learning: Introduction to the Special Issue. *The Elementary School Journal, 112*(3), 409–418. https://doi.org/10.1086/663297

Schultz, K., & Fecho, B. (2000). Society's child: Social context and writing development. *Educational Psychologist, 35*(1), 51–62. https://doi.org/10.1207/S15326985EP3501_6

Sessions, L., Kang, M. O., & Womack, S. (2016). The neglected "R": Improving writing instruction through iPad Apps. *TechTrends, 60*(3), 218–225. https://doi.org/10.1007/s11528-016-0041-8

Shin, D. S. (2018). Multimodal mediation and argumentative writing: A case study of a multilingual writer's metalanguage awareness development. In R. Harman (Ed.), *Bilingual learners and social equity: Critical approaches to systemic functional linguistics* (pp. 225–242). New York: Springer.

Shin, D. S., Cimasko, T., & Yi, Y. (2020). Development of metalanguage for multimodal composing: A case study of an L2 writer's design of multimedia texts. *Journal of Second Language Writing, 47*(1), 7–21. https://doi.org/10.1016/j.jslw.2020.100714

Short, D., & Fitzsimmons, S. (2007). *Double the work: Challenges and solutions for acquiring language and academic literacy for adolescent English language learners.* Report to Carnegie Corporation of New York. New York: Alliance for Excellent Education. https://production-carnegie.s3.amazonaws.com/filer_public/bd/d8/bdd80ac7-fb48-4b97-b082-df8c49320acb/ccny_report_2007_double.pdf

Skerrett, A. (2013). Building multiliterate and multilingual writing practices and identities. *English Education, 45*(4), 322–360.

Smith, B. E., Pacheco, M., & de Almeida, C. R. (2017). Multimodal codemeshing: Bilingual adolescents' processes composing across modes and languages. *Journal of Second Language Writing, 36*, 6–22. https://doi.org/10.1016/j.jslw.2017.04.001

Smith, B. E., Pacheco, M. B., & Khorosheva, M. (2021). Emergent bilingual students and digital multimodal composition: A systematic review of research in secondary classrooms. *Reading Research Quarterly, 56*(1), 33–52. https://doi.org/10.1002/rrq.298

Snow, C. E., & Uccelli, P. (2009). The challenge of academic language. In D. R. Olson & N. Torrance (Eds.), *The Cambridge handbook of literacy* (pp. 112–133). New York: Cambridge University Press.

Vanek, J., King, K., & Bigelow, M. (2018). Social presence and identity: Facebook in an English language classroom. *Journal of Language, Identity & Education, 17*(4), 236–254. https://doi.org/10.1080/15348458.2018.1442223

Villalva, K. E. (2006). Hidden literacies and inquiry approaches of bilingual high school writers. *Written Communication, 23*(1), 91–129. https://doi.org/10.1177/0741088305283929

Vu, V., Warschaure, M., & Yim, S. (2019). Digital storytelling: A district initiative for academic literacy improvement. *Journal of Adolescent & Adult Literacy, 63*(3), 257–267. https://doi.org/10.1002/jaal.962

Walsh, C. S. (2009). The multi-modal redesign of school texts. *Journal of Research in Reading*, *32*(1), 126–136. https://doi.org/10.1111/j.1467-9817.2008.01385.x

Wilcox, K. C. (2011). Writing across the curriculum for secondary school English language learners: A case study. *Writing & Pedagogy*, *3*(1), 79–111. https://doi.org/10.1558/wap.v3i1.79

Wilcox, K. C., & Jeffery, J. V. (2015). Adolescent English language learners' stances toward disciplinary writing. *English for Specific Purposes*, *38*, 44–56. https://doi.org/10.1016/j.esp.2014.11.006

Wilcox, K. C., Yagelski, R., & Yu, F. (2014). The nature of error in adolescent student writing. *Reading & Writing*, *27*(6), 1073–1094. http://dx.doi.org/10.17239/jowr-2015.07.01.02

Williams, C., & Beam, S. (2019). Technology and writing: Review of research. *Computers & Education*, *128*, 227–242. https://doi.org/10.1016/j.compedu.2018.09.024

Wilson, A. A., Chavez, K., & Anders, P. L. (2012). "From the *Koran and family guy*": expressions of identity in English learners' digital podcasts. *Journal of Adolescent & Adult Literacy*, *55*(5), 374–384. https://doi.org/10.1002/JAAL.00046

Yi, Y. (2010). Identity matters: Theories that help explore adolescent multilingual writers and their identities. In M. Cox, J. Jordan, C. Ortmeier-Hooper & G. Schwartz (Eds.), *Reinventing identities in second language* (pp. 303–324). Urbana Champaign, IL: National Council of Teachers of English.

Yi, Y. (2013). Adolescent multilingual writer's negotiation of multiple identities and access to academic writing: A case study of a Jogi Yuhak student in an American high school. *Canadian Modern Language Review*, *69*(2), 207–231. https://doi.org/10.3138/cmlr.1381

Yi, Y., Shin, D. S., & Cimasko, T. (2019). Multimodal literacies in teaching and learning English. In L. de Oliveira (Ed.), *Handbook of TESOL in K-12* (pp. 163–178). Hoboken, NJ: Wiley Blackwell.

5 Reconceptualizing the Connections between In-School and Out-of-School Literate Lives
A Symbiotic Approach

Introduction

In the previous two chapters (Chapters 3 and 4), I focused on discussing out-of-school and academic writing practices of adolescent multilingual students in separate manners. Chapter 3 explained defining characteristics of out-of-school writing (e.g., self-initiated, voluntary, intentional, interest-driven, peer-driven, and multilingual) and illustrated ways in which young people write, communicate, learn, and represent themselves through out-of-school writing, whereas Chapter 4 focused more on the issues with school-sponsored, academic writing to better understand academic writing experiences and expectations of adolescent multilingual students. Drawing upon the discussions in these chapters, this chapter attempts to put them together, discussing how the connections between in-school and out-of-school writing have been conceptualized in the literature, from earlier conversations to more recent and critical ones. Most importantly, based on these discussions and conceptualizations, I propose an expanded perspective of the connections, or what I term a symbiotic approach, which emphasizes exploring and fostering bi-directional relationships between the two. From this chapter on, I attempt to expand my discussion to writing and literacy practices because the conversations about the connections between in-school and out-of-school writing, including a symbiotic approach, can be more broadly applied to writing and literacy research and pedagogy.

Earlier Conversations about the Connections

Since Shirley Brice Heath's (1983) classic study of children learning to use language and literacy at school and at home, literacy scholars, especially those from sociocultural perspectives, have examined and theorized about the nature of writing and literacy across various social contexts (Lankshear, Gee, Knobel, & Searle, 1997; Street, 1984). Continuing in this tradition, studies have documented students' engagement in rich and diverse writing practices outside of school, such as at home, in after-school programs, in community centers, and on the Internet. Likewise, a growing number of scholars have explored the connections and disconnections between young people's out-of-school writing practices and academic writing practices required to perform in school (Black, 2005; Li, 2007; McCarthey, 1997; Moje et al., 2004). For instance, from five elementary school students of diverse backgrounds in the United States, McCarthey (1997) found that home-school connections were stronger for some students than for others. The connections were tight for middle-class European-American students who tended to bring items and writing from home to school to share with peers, whereas students from non-mainstream backgrounds experienced school and home as separate because their home literacy activities did not quite match school experiences. Similarly, from the homes of two Chinese immigrant families in Canada, Li (2007) found great linguistic and cultural discontinuities between Chinese-Canadian children's school and home language/literacy experiences and expectations. Overall, the discontinuities profoundly influenced their language and literacy learning (e.g., resulting in a participant's slow progress in English).

In general, earlier conversations about the connections between the two centered on the differences between in-school and out-of-school writing and literacy practices that some call, *home-school mismatch*, which is considered "the most resilient theme in the two last decades of New Literacy Studies" (Maybin, 2007, p. 516). These studies have suggested pedagogical implications of how to capitalize on students' out-of-school writing and literacy *for* academic achievement. Educators have implemented bridging activities through which students can mobilize their out-of-school experiences and resources into classroom practices.

More Recent and Critical Conversations about the Connections

Although earlier research on the (dis)connections between in-school and out-of-school writing practices has yielded significant knowledge, a group of more recent literacy scholars has engaged in deeper and more critical conversations about how to conceptualize these connections. One of the major criticisms of earlier studies was that the literature on multiple literacies and the connections between in-school and out-of-school writing emphasized the differences and discontinuities between the two and, thus, often presented them as discrete and being in stark contrast to each other (Villalva, 2006). Some even described it as the home-school mismatch or incongruence. However, this could promote a deficit perspective of students and their out-of-school writing and literacy through which the school may attempt to reinforce its view onto families whose literacy practices do not match school experiences and expectations (Kajee, 2011).

In addition, a growing number of literacy scholars (Alvermann & Moore, 2011; Grote, 2006; Hull & Schultz, 2002; Orellana & Reynolds, 2008; Yi, 2010) have pointed out the risk of having "a simplistic and dichotomized view of the relation between literacy practices in and out of school" (Hultin & Westman, 2018, p. 520). Literacy scholars, while questioning the separation of in-school and out-of-school writing contexts, have challenged the dichotomy. Alvermann and Moore (2011) challenged the premise that "the divide between in- and out-of-school literacy learning is real and, as such, needs bridging" and "the common assumption that the type of literacy learning that takes place in each locale is qualitatively different" (p. 156). These scholars have collectively underscored interrelations between in-school and out-of-school writing and literacy, contesting the dichotomous view.

These challenges have been supported by empirical evidence that has shown young people engage in informal out-of-school writing practices alongside school-sponsored academic writing activities, while swiftly moving between the two activities (Björkvall & Engblom, 2010; Hultin & Westman, 2018; Ranker, 2009). Hultin and Westman (2018), based on young children's writing practices at school and at home in Sweden, argued that these children engaged in a "hybridization process" in which varied semiotic resources from different writing practices interplay (p. 518). These students' in-school and out-of-school writing practices often took place in almost a simultaneous and hybridized manner. Similarly, Grote's (2006) study of multilingual Indigenous teenage girls in Australia revealed that their unofficial practices outside of school seeped into official, academic writing practices in the classroom (e.g., including inappropriate language in the journal task). They also infused unofficial content into school tasks (e.g., researching hip hop celebrities as an admired person for a school project, integrating hip hop themes into literacy tasks, and drawing on graffiti for school-issued materials during class) and embedded teen writing styles (e.g., embedding informal abbreviation, like "INFO" and colloquial language like "stuff") in academic tasks.

These girls' unofficial writing practices outside of school permeated the boundaries of school-sponsored writing practices, which suggests that "the boundaries between them [school-sponsored and vernacular literacies] are subject to transgression" (p. 478). All these findings collectively suggest that "it is almost impossible to eliminate overlapping literacy practices and learning." (Alvermann & Moore, 2011, p. 156). In this vein, some scholars have argued for deconstructing the "boundaries between classroom and community" (Moje, Collazo, Carrillo, & Marx, 2001, p. 492) and disrupting "the compartmentalization of literacy practices" multilingual children face across the home and the school contexts (Cañas et al., 2018, p. 301).

While challenging a simple dichotomous view of the relationship between the two writing practices and contexts, scholars have further conceptualized their connections. One group of scholars have focused more on exploring the commonalities, continuities, and convergence between the two (Bulfin & Koutsogiannis, 2012; Leurs & Ponzanesi, 2011; McLean, 2010) and place all the writing practices on a continuum, which can provide a more comprehensive view of students' writing and literacy (Cañas et al., 2018).

Another group of scholars have been interested in examining and discussing the tensions and conflicts that adolescent writers and their teachers face in their attempts to better understand and conceptualize the connections between in-school and out-of-school writing and literacy (de la Piedra, 2010; Dickie, 2011; Enright, 2014; Enright & Wong, 2018; Haddix & Williams, 2016). Enright (2014) has directly addressed tensions and conflicts that adolescent multilingual students experience. She asserts that the field of L2 writing and literacy is faced with a perplexing contradiction and needs to reconcile tensions. More specifically, the writing curriculum in secondary school is narrowing and more prescriptive (e.g., writing assignments tailored to prepare for high-stakes writing tests), but young people need to be prepared to engage in a wide range of new writing and literacy practices for a global economy. In fact, classroom teachers can exacerbate the tensions that students feel because they emphasize certain types of writing (e.g., argumentative and informative) that are privileged by standardized curricula and count them as official and legitimate, and unfortunately overlook other types of writing that could be more meaningful and relevant to students beyond their classroom contexts. Interestingly, some teachers themselves often struggle with "conflicts between the goals of meaningful literacy instruction and the narrow definition of school literacy practices that derived from standardized testing practices" (de la Piedra, 2010, p. 581).

In summary, empirical evidence and theoretical discussions of the connections between in-school and out-of-school writing practices and contexts have contributed to advancing the conceptualization of the connections between the two. Yet, all the discussions tend to center on how to use out-of-school writing for the development of academic writing in the classroom, which is understandable. However, this tendency could lead us to overlook the value of out-of-school writing on its own. Additionally, little has been discussed about how academic writing practice and experience can positively impact young people's out-of-school literate lives. While problematizing such a one-way scholarly attention to exploring how to capitalize on out-of-school experiences *for* academic success, I propose an alternative conceptualization of the connections by highlighting mutually beneficial, two-way relationships between the two, which is elaborated in the subsequent section.

A Symbiotic Approach to the Connections between In-School and Out-of-School Literate Lives

As I have discussed so far, literacy researchers have examined and discussed how in-school and out-of-school writing and literacy practices, experiences, and knowledge are (dis)connected. Yet, they still face the challenge of an "undertheorized relationship" between literacies across out-of-school (home) and in-school contexts (Bulfin & Koutsogiannisb, 2012, p. 334). Developing more nuanced accounts of the relationship between in-school and out-of-school writing and literacy learning will help literacy scholars reconceptualize adolescent (multilingual) literacy, which is one of the aims of this book. Drawing upon empirical evidence and theoretical discussions from existing literature, I propose and call for a symbiotic approach to examine and cultivate the connections between in-school and out-of-school writing and literacy. Essentially, I try to expand our inquiries from "How to mobilize out-of-school literacy experience, knowledge, and resources for in-school academic literacy?" to "How to cultivate mutually beneficial relationships between the two literacy practices and contexts?" In this section, I elaborate several core ideas of a symbiotic approach, which can be more broadly applied to literacy research and pedagogy.

Cultivating Mutually Beneficial and Bidirectional Relationships

When researchers and practitioners discuss the connections or relationships between adolescents' in-school and out-of-school literacy practices and contexts, they should pay careful attention to the bidi-rectional relationships between them. In other words, they should explore how adolescents' academic literacy learning influences their out-of-school literate lives and vice versa. As I have noted several times, the majority of empirical research and pedagogical suggestions about connecting in-school and out-of-school literate experiences and envi-ronments seem to directly address or indirectly imply that research-ers and practitioners need to figure out how they can and should use students' out-of-school experiences and resources *for* academic writing and literacy practices. For instance, pedagogical recommendations in the literature encourage teachers to (1) leverage students' "funds of knowledge" (Dickie, 2011; Marshall & Toohey, 2010; Moll & González, 2004; Orellana & Reynolds, 2008), including heritage language and cul-ture (Souryasack & Lee, 2007) and pop culture (de la Piedra, 2010); (2) create a "third space" (Daniel, 2018; Moje et al., 2004; Wiltse, 2015); and (3) implement "bridging or linking" activities (Danzak, 2011; Hull & Schultz, 2002; Pyo, 2016), such as "critical literacy" (Haneda, 2006), "hybrid literacies" (Smythe & Toohey, 2009), and "translanguaging" practices (Daniel, 2018). These recommendations provide significant means to capitalize on adolescents' rich, diverse, and meaningful out-of-school experiences for academic literacy learning. In a similar vein, a recent review article (Vaughan, 2019) conceptualizes scholarship on adolescents' out-of-school writing by exploring a guiding question, "How can K–12 educators use the existing literature on adolescent out-of-school writing in their curricula?" (p. 529). As such, when researchers and practitioners seek to make powerful and meaningful connections between the two, it is almost by default to consider out-of-school writing and literacy to enhance formal, academic literacy learning. Perhaps, it is an understandable effort given that research has constantly reported that "mainstream schools failed to recognize the importance of these diverse home literacy activities, thus showing little support for them, or even strong opposition" (Dixon & Wu, 2014, p. 432). Furthermore, many multilingual students with rich real-world life and literacy expe-riences can be easily silenced in their classroom (Bauer et al., 2017). In this sense, it is significant to connect the two while highlighting the importance of developing academic writing and literacy.

However, this one-way connection is insufficient to obtain a compre-hensive picture of adolescent (multilingual) literacy. Researchers and practitioners must think hard about whether, to what extent (if any), and how students' academic literacy experiences can positively and productively influence their out-of-school literate lives now and later in their lives. About 15 years ago, Pugh and Bergin (2005) synthesized existing research on the effect of schooling on students' out-of-school experience and found that little research had investigated the influence of school learning on out-of-school experience. Based on the analysis of a small number of such studies, they concluded that "school learning has less of an influence on out-of-school experience than we would hope for and expect" (p. 21).

In the field of writing and literacy, a small group of scholars have more recently acknowledged and explicitly pointed out that "a critical function of schooling is to provide young writers with opportunities to explore real-life, out-of-school experiences through writing" (Bauer, Presiado, & Colomer, 2017, p. 10), although little is known about the impact of academic writing upon out-of-school literate lives. I was able to locate only a handful of studies (McTavish, 2014; Yancey et al., 2019) as examples of investigating the influence of academic writing upon students' out-of-school literate lives, although, these studies did not necessarily examine multilingual students. McTavish (2014), while documenting a Canadian second grade student's literacy practices in academic and out-of-school contexts, tried to address "What young children do with the literacies they have learned at school? and How school literacy may impact on some children's out-of-school literacies?" (p. 319). This study seems to be the only research that directly addresses how academic literacy influences students' out-of-school literacies. McTavish found that the focal child, Tara, recontextualized academic literacy in out-of-school contexts and even changed it in more flexible, playful, and technologically-mediated manners. For instance, Tara recontextualized mapping skills learned in class to the context of playing a computer game at home by designing a virtual bedroom in the game. Similarly, the spelling skills learned in the class were recontextualized and used when playing a computer game as well. Unlike almost all the out-of-school literacy studies, McTavish (2014) made a unique suggestion that "It seems more realistic to concentrate efforts on supporting those out-of-school contexts that enable children to recontextualize school practices for wider and more global use" (p. 337).

In a slightly different study, Yancey et al. (2019) documented how college students in writing courses at four different American universities transferred writing knowledge and practice concurrently into other contexts of writing (e.g., other college courses, workplaces). They found that when college students understood that "appropriate transfer of writing knowledge and practices is both possible and desirable, they transferred from in-school contexts into out-of-school contexts with facility" (p. 268). For instance, a participant, Teresa, transferred her writing knowledge and practice from the upper-level writing course to an out-of-school workplace writing context (e.g., as marketing coordinator for a community college). She drew on the key terms learned in the class (e.g., audience, genre, context, purpose, and rhetorical situation) to frame many of her out-of-school writing situations (e.g., writing marketing materials to reach a wide audience). Findings from these two studies help rethink how to prepare young people to meet the writing demands in their everyday lives as well as for their future opportunities.

Finally, unlike the studies that looked into one-way relationships, there are a few studies that examined the potentially bidirectional relationships between in-school and out-of-school literacy learning (e.g., Bulfin & Koutsogiannis, 2012; Rothoni, 2018; Yi, 2010). Within L1 literacy research, Bulfin and Koutsogiannis (2012) explored how school-authorized technology practices of secondary students in Greece and Australia mediated out-of-school digital literacy practices and vice versa. With the focus on students' use of digital media, this research delimited the conversations surrounding the relationships between their digital literacies in and out of school. Both Greek and Australian adolescent students demonstrated that their experience with school literacy played an important mediating role in their out-of-school ways with information and communications technology (ICT), and thus, connections and continuity existed between in-school and out-of-school digital literacy practices (e.g., practicing word processing and creating computer animations using programs like Adobe Flash). For instance, Tania, an Australian teen, did not necessarily enjoy school-authorized practices, yet some, like learning to program Flash, gave her a "point of connection and engagement with her own interests" outside of school (p. 341). Here the students used academic writing and literacy "as a basis from which to reexplore their own interests" outside of school (p. 344).

Within L2 studies, Lai (2015) and Kashiwa and Benson (2018) examined college students' perceptions about the relationship between in-school and out-of-school second or foreign language learning experiences. These studies had not necessarily examined writing or literacy experiences, but rather focused on exploring college students' language learning experiences more globally from their perspectives. What is important here is that both studies took the bidirectional approach by examining how their in-school learning shaped their out-of-school learning experiences and vice versa. Interestingly, participating learners of foreign languages (e.g., German and Korean) in Hong Kong (Lai, 2015) perceived in-school and out-of-school language learning as complementary, allocating different functions to language learning (e.g., out-of-school learning as serving "social and motivational functions" and in-school learning affording "cognitive and metacognitive functions") (p. 275). Slightly differently, Asian English learners in the university English Language Center in Sydney, Australia (Kashiwa & Benson, 2018) perceived in-school and out-of-school learning as more integrated with each other while "seeing opportunities for a bidirectional transfer of language content and skills and learning in the classroom stimulating learning outside the classroom, and vice versa" (p. 742).

Beyond the studies on student perceptions, only a very few studies have examined how adolescent multilingual students actually established bidirectional relationships between in-school and out-of-school writing and literacy practices (Rothoni, 2018; Yi, 2010). Both Rothoni's (2018) and Yi's (2010) studies revealed the blurred boundary between the two by examining the complex relationship between formal, in-school and informal, out-of-school literacy practices. In Rothoni's research of Greek teenagers who learn English as a foreign language, informal texts and practices in English traversed across home and school. Their school-related academic practices were infiltrated into the home, influencing their English literacy practices in out-of-school settings (e.g., reading English novels in free time for the purpose of improving English); additionally, their home or vernacular literacies were used at school (e.g., writing English lyrics on a school handout). While Rothoni's research was conducted in an EFL context, Yi's (2010) study was conducted in an ESL context. Jihee, a Korean immigrant high school student in the United States, significantly drew upon her out-of-school writing (especially, diary writing that was mostly in Korean with some English mixed in) for her Creative Writing class. At the same time, her in-school writing activities and assignments were extensively mentioned in her out-of-school writing practices. Jihee's writing activities across the two contexts were greatly influenced by each other, especially with respect to the topics, genres, and languages of the writing practices. Findings from both Rothoni's and Yi's research demonstrate that writing practices across the two contexts can be mutually supportive, not mutually exclusive. These findings suggest that it is important to explore and cultivate mutually beneficial and bidirectional relationships between students' in-school and out-of-school literate lives.

Equally Legitimate Practices

Another core idea of a symbiotic approach to the connections between academic and out-of-school writing and literacy is to acknowledge that both are equally legitimate, with each serving different functions or purposes in young people's lives. As I noted in Chapter 3, the L2 writing field "does not seem terribly interested in how individuals go about writing social, professional, or workplace genres" (Hyland, 2013, p. 426). In addition, students' out-of-school writing experience and knowledge have remained unnoticed, invisible, and undervalued in the classroom as they are less included in the curricula (Haddix, 2018). Teachers may not value students' out-of-school writing; some may treat it as "frivolous" and "leisure-time pursuits" (Black, 2009 p. 696). However, out-of-school writing is as powerful as academic writing, if not more, as I have demonstrated throughout Chapter 3. Adolescent multilingual students tend to negotiate their interests, identities, and other important issues at the crossroads of linguistic, cultural, ethnic, and racial specificities among others through out-of-school writing and literacy practices. Given that, researchers and practitioners should consider both academic and out-of-school writing and literacy as equally legitimate, sanctioned, and respectful. This perspective should be the foundation for a symbiotic approach to the connections between in-school and out-of-school literate lives.

In order to treat in-school and out-of-school writing and literacy practices as equally legitimate, I argue that out-of-school writing and literacy should be understood and examined on their own. They should not be considered as secondary or supplementary to in-school academic writing and literacy. Perhaps acknowledging the value of out-of-school writing on its own, as well as treating academic and out-of-school literacy as equally legitimate in adolescents' lives, could be quite provocative to some researchers and practitioners. Yet, without such an alternative perspective, the explorations and understandings of adolescent literacy will still remain partial.

Attention to Layering Writing Practices

When I discuss the mutually beneficial and supportive relationships between in-school and out-of-school writing and literacy above, I focus more on a two-way influence between the two. Here I want to highlight the fact that adolescents layer writing and engage in meaning-making across multiple contexts. The notion of layering writing practices emphasizes fluid and moving practices and interaction within and across in-school and out-of-school writing practices and contexts, considering "multiple entry points and directionalities" (Abrams & Russo, 2015, p. 131). Layering writing practices is especially compelling to consider when in-school and out-of-school writing boundaries are more permeable. I draw upon this concept of "layering" from Abrams and Russo (2015). According to them, "layering" writing and literacy refers to

> the ways that combinations of digital and nondigital practices, texts, and spaces work in concert to support meaning making; such layering is not linear in fashion, nor is it a simple or tidy accumulation of practices. Rather, it includes multidirectional and often irregular movement and interaction among and across experiences, texts, and modalities (p. 132).

As readers may know, many young people move fluidly among their writing activities as they negotiate different types of texts, modes, and formats. For instance, Mike, an 11th grade transnational teen, who traveled back and forth between the United States and South Korea, logged onto instant messaging, checked emails, played music, and read articles on his interests (e.g., video games, music albums, and basketball games). Oftentimes, he did his homework sitting before his computer while responding to sporadic instant messages from his friends (Yi, 2009). In a more recent study (Smith, Pacheco, & de Almeida, 2017), Yuliana, a Spanish-English bilingual 8th grader, navigated various modes and media (including written words in English and Spanish, images, voice recordings, background music, and slide animations) to create her "My Hero" project, which was a multimodal presentation on her personal hero. Her project focused on her mother's heroic journey from El Salvador to the United States. Despite her limited English proficiency, Yuliana constantly traversed text, images, sound, and movement modes while searching and editing images (using English and Spanish), writing presentation slides, editing the writing on the slides, inserting transitions, and using her cultural and out-of-school knowledge during the in-class workshop. One important aspect to point out here is that adolescents, like Yuliana, may voluntarily "seek and discover relationships between in-school and out-of-school learning when boundaries are permeable" (Abrams & Russo, 2015, p. 134). Paying attention to adolescents' layering of writing and literacy is another core element of a symbiotic approach to the connections between in-school and out-of-school literate lives.

Considering Student Perspectives

It is also important to consider how students actually think of the connections between in-school and out-of-school literate lives. When researchers and practitioners conceptualize the connections, they should not simply assume that students would be interested in or poor at making the connections or crossing the boundaries between them. Often students do not perceive their out-of-school literacy engagement as useful or important for their academic practices, although they find it appealing and meaningful (e.g., Yi, Kao, & Kang, 2017). In other words, some language learners may see in-school and out-of-school practices rather parallel (e.g., foreign language learners at a New Zealand university in Alm's study in 2015), and thus they do not feel the need for connecting or bridging the practices and contexts. In addition, others may be reluctant to connect or combine their out-of-school literacy (e.g., Facebook practice) with their school-related practices (e.g., secondary school students in Italy in Manca and Grion in 2017). Anecdotally speaking, some students believe that the moment they bring their out-of-school writing to the classroom, all the fun aspects disappear. Similarly, some out-of-school literacy scholars have warned teachers that "coopting adolescents' out-of-school literacy practices for classroom learning disrespects and defeats the purposes for which youth engage in them [out-of-school literacy practices]" (Skerrett & Bomer, 2011, p. 1261). Overall, students' perspectives of the connections between the two, which have been underexplored, can contribute to cultivating a symbiotic relationship. The perspectives of the most important stakeholders, students, need to be considered. Furthermore, in-depth understandings of students' perceptions of their own literacy practices, their own sense of the value of writing/literacy, and their views of themselves as writers and learners can deepen understandings about adolescent writing and literacy.

Sharing Responsibility

Finally, one of the core ideas of a symbiotic approach to the connections between in-school and out-of-school writing and literacy is that we need to reinforce the idea that helping adolescents be and become competent writers and literate beings is a shared responsibility among researchers, practitioners, policy makers, family, community, students, and so on. In particular, two groups – educators and family members – are especially crucial ones for adolescent writing and literacy learning and practices. If they had each known *what, how*, and *why* the other was teaching and engaging students with writing and literacy, then both groups would have been much more productive and effective to educate and raise competent readers and writers. In addition, these two groups need to keep questioning *whether, how* (if any), and *to what extent* students' writing and literacy engagement in one context influences literate lives in another. As it takes a village to raise a child, it takes a village to raise a (multi)literate child.

Summary

In order to expand the understanding of the nature of adolescent writing and literacy, literacy scholars have explored students' out-of-school literacy practices and experiences in relation to their academic literacy. In this line of inquiry, researches and practitioners have been interested in investigating and fostering possible connections between students' in-school and out-of-school literate lives. Despite significant knowledge generated by their efforts, theoretical discussions and pedagogical practices have been rather one dimensional, figuring out how to capitalize on out-of-school experiences *for* academic literacy development required in school. Little research has examined the impact of academic literacy upon out-of-school literacy. We have not engaged in critical discussions around whether, to what extent (if any), and how students' academic literacy experiences positively influence their literate lives beyond the classroom. Problematizing this one-way scholarly attention to the use of out-of-school experiences for academic literacy learning, I propose an alternative perspective of the connections between in-school and out-of-school writing, or what I term a symbiotic approach to the connections. This approach to the connections strives to (a) cultivate mutually beneficial, two-way relationships between in-school and out-of-school literate lives, (b) acknowledge both literacy practices as equally legitimate, (c) pay attention to layering of writing and literacy practices, (d) consider student perspectives of connections and literacy, and (e) improve students' literate lives through shared responsibility. This symbiotic approach to these connections can eventually allow for a comprehensive understanding and reconceptualization of adolescent writing and literacy.

References

Abrams, S. S., & Russo, M. (2015). Layering literacies in the classroom. *Journal of Adolescent & Adult Literacy*, 59(2), 131–135. https://doi.org/10.1002/jaal.447
Alm, A. (2015). Facebook for informal language learning: Perspectives from tertiary language students. *The EUROCALL Review*, 23(2), 3–18.
Alvermann, D., & Moore, D. (2011). Questioning the separation of in-school from out-of-school contexts for literacy learning: An interview with Donna E. Alvermann. *Journal of Adolescent & Adult Literacy*, 55(2), 156–158. https://doi.org/10.1002/JAAL.00019

Bauer, E. B., Presiado, V., & Colomer, S. (2017). Writing through partnership: How emergent bilinguals foster translanguaging. *Journal of Literacy Research, 49*(1), 10–37. https://doi.org/10.1177/1086296X16683417

Björkvall, A., & Engblom, C. (2010). Young children's exploration of semiotic resources during unofficial computer activities in the classroom. *Journal of Early Childhood Literacy, 10* (3), 271–293. https://doi.org/10.1177/1468798410372159

Black, R. W. (2005). Access and affiliation: The literacy and composition practices of English–language learners in an online facfiction community. *Journal of Adolescent and Adult Literacy, 49*(2), 118–128. https://doi.org/10.1598/JAAL.49.2.4

Black, R. W. (2009). Online fan fiction, global identities, and imagination. *Research in the Teaching of English, 43*(4), 397–425.

Bulfin, S. A., & Koutsogiannis, D. (2012). New literacies as multiply placed practices: Expanding perspectives on young people's literacies across home and school. *Language & Education, 26*(4), 331–346. https://doi.org/10.1080/09500782.2012.691515

Cañas, C., Ocampo, A. P., Rodriguez, A. K., Lopez-Ladino, M., & Mora, R. A. (2018). Toward a participatory view of early literacies in second language contexts: A reflection on research from Colombia. In G. Onchwari & J. Keengwe (Eds.), *Handbook of research on pedagogies and cultural considerations for young English language learners* (pp. 300–324). Hershey, PA: IGI Global. https://doi.org/10.4018/978-1-5225-7507-8.ch018

Daniel, S. (2018). Resettled refugee youth leveraging their out-of-school literacy practices to accomplish schoolwork. *Mind, Culture, and Activity, 25*(3), 263–277. https://doi.org/10.1080/10749039.2018.1481092

Danzak, R. (2011). Defining identities through multiliteracies: EL teens narrate their immigration experiences as graphic stories. *Journal of Adolescent & Adult Literacy, 55*(3), 187–196. https://doi.org/10.1002/JAAL.00024

de la Piedra, M. T. (2010). Adolescent worlds and literacy practices on the United States–Mexico border. *Journal of Adolescent & Adult Literacy, 53*(7), 575–584. https://doi.org/10.1598/JAAL.53.7.5

Dickie, J. G. (2011). Samoan students documenting their out-of-school literacies: An insider view on conflicting values. *Australian Journal of Language and Literacy, 34*(3), 247–259.

Dixon, L. Q., & Wu, S. (2014). Home language and literacy practices among immigrant second-language learners. *Language Teaching, 47*(4), 414–449. https://doi.org/10.1017/S0261444814000160

Enright, K. A. (2014). Standards and personalization in the writing of linguistically diverse students. *Writing & Pedagogy, 6*(1), 59–88. https://doi.org/10.1558/wap.v6i1.59

Enright, K. A., & Wong, J. W. (2018). Relocalizing standards in English language arts: Consequences on functions of literacy. *Critical Inquiry in Language Studies, 15*(2), 85–114. https://doi.org/10.1080/15427587.2017.1338957

Grote, E. (2006). Challenging the boundaries between school-sponsored and vernacular literacies: Urban indigenous teenage girls writing in an "at risk" programme. *Language & Education, 20*, 478–492. https://doi.org/10.2167/le659.0

Haddix, M. M. (2018). Writing our lives: Preparing teachers to teach 21st century writers in and out of school. In K. Zenkov & K. E. Pytash (Eds.), *Clinical experiences in teacher education* (pp.137–152). New York: Routledge.

Haddix, M. M. & Williams, B. (2016). Who's coming to the composition classroom?: K-12 writing in and outside the context of common core state standards. In N. Welch & T. Scott (Eds.), *Composition in the age of austerity* (pp. 65–74). Boulder, CO: University Press of Colorado. https://doi.org/10.7330/9781607324454.c004

Haneda, M. (2006). Becoming literate in a second language: Connecting home, community, and school literacy practices. *Theory into Practice, 45*(4), 337–345. https://doi.org/10.1207/s15430421tip4504_7

Heath, S. B. (1983). *Ways with words: Language, life, and work in communities and classrooms*. Cambridge, UK: Cambridge University Press.

Hull, G. A., & Schultz, K. (Eds.). (2002). *School's out: Bridging out-of-school literacies with classroom practice*. New York, NY: Teachers College Press.

Hultin, E., & Westman, M. (2018). The reuse of semiotic resources in third-year children's writing of sub-genres. *Journal of Early Childhood Literacy, 18*(4), 518–544. https://doi.org/10.1177/1468798416685768

Hyland, K. (2013). Second language writing: The manufacture of a social fact. *Journal of Second Language Writing, 22*(4), 426–427. http://dx.doi.org/10.1016/j.jslw.2013.08.001

Kajee, L. (2011). Multimodal representation of identity in the English-as-an-additional-language classroom in South Africa. *Language, Culture, & Curriculum, 24*(3), 241–252. https://doi.org/10.1080/07908318.2011.610896

Kashiwa, M., & Benson, P. (2018). A road and a forest: Conceptions of in-class and out-of-class learning in the transition to study abroad. *TESOL Quarterly, 52*(4), 725–747. https://doi.org/10.1002/tesq.409

Lai, C. (2015). Perceiving and traversing in-class and out-of-class learning: Accounts from foreign language learners in Hong Kong. *Innovation in Language Learning and Teaching, 9*(3), 265–284. https://doi.org/10.1080/17501229.2014.918982

Lankshear, C., Gee, J. P., Knobel, M., & Searle, C. (1997). *Changing literacies*. Buckingham: Open University Press.

Leurs, K., & Ponzanesi, S. (2011). Communicative spaces of their own: Migrant girls performing selves using instant messaging software. *Feminist Review, 99*(1), 55–78. https://doi.org/10.1057/fr.2011.39

Li, G. (2007). Second language and literacy learning in school and at home: An ethnographic study of Chinese-Canadian first graders' experiences. *Journal of Language Teaching and Learning, 11*(1), 1–40.

Manca, S., & Grion, V. (2017). Engaging students in school participatory practice through Facebook: The story of a failure. *British Journal of Educational Technology, 48*(5), 1153–1163. https://doi.org/10.1111/bjet.12527

Marshall, E. & Toohey, K. (2010). Representing family: Community funds of knowledge, bilingualism, and multimodality. *Harvard Educational Review, 80*(2), 221–242. https://doi.org/10.17763/haer.80.2.h3446j54n608q442

Maybin, J. (2007). Literacy under and over the desk: Oppositions and heterogeneity. *Language & Education, 21*(6), 515–530. https://doi.org/10.2167/le720.0

McCarthey, S. J. (1997). Connecting home and school literacy practices in classrooms with diverse populations. *Journal of Literacy Research, 29*, 145–182. https://doi.org/10.1080%2F10862969709547955

McLean, C. A. (2010). A space called home: An immigrant adolescent's digital literacy practices. *Journal of Adolescent & Adult Literacy, 54*(1), 13–22. https://doi.org/10.1598/JAAL.54.1.2

McTavish, M. (2014). "I'll do it my own way!": A young child's appropriation and recontextualization of school literacy practices in out-of-school spaces. *Journal of Early childhood Literacy, 14*(3), 319–344. https://doi.org/10.1177%2F1468798413494919

Moje, E. B., Ciechanowski, K. M., Kramer, K., Ellis, L., Carrillo, R., & Collazo, T. (2004) Working toward third space in content area literacy: An examination of everyday funds of knowledge and discourse. *Reading Research Quarterly, 39*(1), 38–70. https://doi.org/10.1598/RRQ.39.1.4

Moje, E. B., Collazo, T., Carrillo, R., & Marx, R. W. (2001). "Maestro, what is 'quality'?": Language, literacy, and discourse in project-based science. *Journal of Research in Science Teaching, 38*(4), 469–498. https://doi.org/10.1002/tea.1014

Moll, L. C., & González, N. (2004). Engaging life: A funds of knowledge approach to multicultural education. In J. A. Banks & C.A.M. Banks (Eds.), *Handbook of research on multicultural education* (2nd ed., pp. 699–715). San Francisco, CA: Jossey-Bass.

Orellana, M. F., & Reynolds, J. (2008). Cultural modeling: Leveraging bilingual skills for school paraphrasing tasks. *Reading Research Quarterly, 43*(1), 48–65. https://doi.org/10.1598/RRQ.43.1.4

Pugh, K. J., & Bergin, D. A. (2005). The effect of schooling on students' out-of-school experience. *Educational Researcher, 34*(9), 15–23. https://doi.org/10.3102%2F0013189X034009015

Pyo, J. (2016). Bridging in-school and out-of-school literacies an adolescent EL's composition of a multimodal project. *Journal of Adolescent & Adult Literacy, 59*(4), 421–430. https://doi.org/10.1002/jaal.467

Ranker, J. (2009). Student appropriation of writing lessons throng hybrid composing practices: Direct, diffuse, and indirect use of teacher-offered writing tools in an ESL classroom. *Journal of Literacy Research, 41*, 393–431. https://doi.org/10.1080/10862960903340124

Rothoni, A. (2018). The complex relationship between home and school literacy: A blurred boundary between formal and informal English literacy practices of Greek teenagers. *TESOL Quarterly, 52*(2), 331–359. https://doi.org/10.1002/tesq.402

Skerrett, A., & Bomer, R. (2011). Borderzones in adolescents' literacy practices: Connecting out-of-school literacies to the reading curriculum. *Urban Education, 46*(6), 1256–1279. https://doi.org/10.1177/0042085911398920

Smith, B., Pacheco, M., & de Almeida, C. R. (2017). Multimodal codemeshing: Bilingual adolescents' processes composing across modes and languages. *Journal of Second Language Writing, 36*, 6–22. https://doi.org/10.1016/j. jslw.2017.04.001

Smythe, S. & Toohey, K. (2009). Investigating sociohistorical contexts and practices through a community scan: A Canadian Punjabi Sikh example. *Language and Education, 21*(1), 7–57. https://doi.org/10.1080/09500780802152887

Souryasack, R., & Lee, J. S. (2007). Drawing on students' experiences, cultures and languages to develop English language writing: Perspectives from three Lao heritage middle school students. *Heritage Language Journal, 5*(1), 79–97.

Street, B. (1984). *Literacy in theory and practice.* New York: Cambridge University Press.

Vaughan, A. (2019). Conceptualizing scholarship on adolescent out-of-school writing toward more equitable teaching and learning: A literature review. *Journal of Adolescent and Adult Literacy, 63*(5), 529–537. https://doi.org/10.1002/jaal.1009

Villalva, K. E. (2006). Hidden literacies and inquiry approaches of bilingual high school writers. *Written Communication, 23*(1), 91–129. https://doi.org/10.1177/ 0741088305283929

Wiltse, L. (2015). Not just 'sunny days': Aboriginal students connect out-of-school literacy resources with school literacy practices. *Literacy, 49*(2), 60–68. https://doi.org/10.1111/lit.12036

Yancey, K. B., Davis, M., Robertson, L., Taczak, K., & Workman, E. (2019). The teaching for transfer curriculum: The role of concurrent transfer and inside-and outside-school contexts in supporting students' writing development. *College Composition and Communication, 71*(2), 268–295.

Yi, Y. (2009). Adolescent literacy and identity construction among 1.5 generation students: From a transnational perspective. *Journal of Asian Pacific Communication, 19*(1), 100–129. https://doi.org/10.1075/japc.19.1.06yi

Yi, Y. (2010). Adolescent multilingual writers' transitions across in- and out-of-school writing contexts. *Journal of Second Language Writing, 19*(1), 17–32. https://doi.org/10.1016/j.jslw.2009.10.001

Yi, Y., Kao, C., & Kang, J. (2017). Digital multimodal composing practices of adolescent English language learners in an after-school program. In S. Rilling & M. Dantas-Whitney, (Eds.), *TESOL voices: Insider accounts of classroom life* (pp. 49–55). Alexandria, VA: TESOL Press.

6 Moving Toward the Reconceptualization of Adolescent Multilingual Writing

Introduction

Adolescent students engage in a wide range of texts and writing practices across various social contexts for different purposes. In particular, their writing practices outside of school have drastically changed, in terms of types, modes, and degrees, along with the ubiquitous use of technology. Yet, adolescent writing, especially for multilingual students, is still relatively unknown in the fields of L2 writing and adolescent literacy. An in-depth and comprehensive investigation of adolescent multilingual writing is necessary to expand L2 researchers' and practitioners' understandings of its nature and to move toward the reconceptualization of adolescent multilingual literacy. This book addresses the urgent need for more attention to this area of inquiry through research synthesis and discussions about the issues adolescent multilingual students encounter in general (Chapter 1), three dominant theoretical frameworks for adolescent multilingual writing research (Chapter 2), out-of-school and in-school writing of adolescent multilingual students (Chapters 3 and 4), and the connections between in-school and out-of-school writing and literacy practices (Chapter 5). This book makes significant contributions to the existing knowledge of L2 writing and adolescent literacy by expanding the perspectives of literacy and literacy research. This final chapter suggests empirical, methodological, and pedagogical implications for adolescent (multilingual) literacy research and pedagogy.

Contributions to Literacy Research and Pedagogy

Discussions and syntheses of the literature in this book provide an in-depth understanding of the nuanced experiences, challenges, and characteristics of adolescent multilingual writers. They also help illuminate the complex nature of adolescent multilingual writing, especially in terms of negotiating multiple languages, literacies, cultures, identities, and technologies across various social contexts (e.g., classroom, home, community, workplace, and online). This book contributes to advancing research in the fields of L2 writing and literacy studies. Most importantly, the discussions, arguments, and syntheses in this book expand the continuum of literacy research in several significant manners.

The discussions in this book expand the perspectives of literacy and literacy research by (a) highlighting an important but underexplored area, such as out-of-school writing and literacy, (b) proposing a symbiotic approach to the connections of students' in-school and out-of-school literate lives, and (c) paying greater attention to multilingual literacy practices. In doing so, all the discussions collectively help reconceptualize adolescent multilingual writing and adolescent literacy.

First, deeper and more critical understandings of students' out-of-school writing contribute to broadening the perspectives of writing and literacy. Traditionally, many writing and literacy studies, regardless of whether they examine L1 or L2 practices, have emphasized the acquisition of academic writing and literacy in English. Although this emphasis on academic writing and literacy has significantly contributed to the field of literacy studies, this knowledge has provided researchers and practitioners with "only a partial view of how literacy operates in students' lives" (Yi, 2005, p. 73). As extensively discussed in Chapter 3, a growing number of out-of-school writing and literacy studies have revealed adolescents' rich, complex, versatile, and meaningful engagement with multiple literacies and identities. The emphasis on more comprehensive understandings of out-of-school literacy enables researchers to (a) obtain a fuller picture of literacy practices by adolescent students, (b) counter deficit perspectives of adolescent (multilingual) students, and (c) reconceptualize "what counts as writing (literacy)" and "what counts as good writing (literacy)" for adolescent students in the 21st century.

Relating to this point, respecting and valuing students' out-of-school writing on its own, which is one of significant arguments in this book, expands the perspectives of literacy. I argue in this book that students' out-of-school writing should be considered and explored on its own, not as a supplementary resource for academic success. In and of itself, out-of-school writing can broaden the perspectives of literacy by challenging the implicit hierarchy between in-school and out-of-school writing and literacy as well as disrupting deficit perspectives of out-of-school literacy as experienced by many young people.

Second, the symbiotic approach to the connections between students' in-school and out-of-school literacy learning, as proposed in this book, expands the perspectives of literacy and literacy research. Many existing studies typically examine only one aspect, such as either in-school, academic literacy or informal, out-of-school literacy. In addition, when some studies have examined both practices, they have focused on addressing how to capitalize on students' out-of-school literacy practices, experiences, and knowledge *for* academic writing and literacy development. Although I acknowledge such significant research endeavors and knowledge generated by those studies, I have pointed out how little investigation has been rigorously conducted on how adolescents' academic writing and literacy experiences influence their out-of-school literate lives. Both researchers and practitioners have not engaged in sufficient and explicit conversations about how students' academic literacy learning matters to their out-of-school literate lives. In this sense, the proposed symbiotic approach to examining and cultivating mutually beneficial, bidirectional relationships between in-school and out-of-school literate lives can expand our perspectives of literacy and deepen our understanding of its nature.

In addition, the symbiotic approach can provide a significant conceptual framework for literacy research and pedagogy, regardless of whether it is about L1 or L2 writing and literacy. By looking into the connections between in-school and out-of-school writing and literacy in a bidirectional manner, the symbiotic approach enables researchers to obtain a more comprehensive picture of how one practice influences the other and how both can be positively connected. Additionally, the symbiotic approach can also be a powerful conceptual framework for pedagogy. This can be accomplished by providing practitioners with guidelines to understand students' literate practices in a fuller manner, facilitating the connections between in-school and out-of-school learning, and reflecting how educators' in-class writing instruction will impact students' out-of-school literate lives and vice versa.

Third, the discussions about multilingual students' writing and literacy in this book can expand the perspective of and enrich the conversation about adolescent literacy. As readers may be aware, K-12 classrooms in Anglophone countries like Australia, Canada, the United Kingdom, and the United States have embraced more and more linguistically diverse, multilingual students. In the context of the United States, approximately 10.1% of public-school students in the fall of 2017 were identified as English learners (ELs) according to the annual report (Condition of Education 2020, May 19). One of the clear patterns of the EL population in the United States is a higher percentage of ELs in lower grades than in upper grades (e.g., approximately 16% of Kindergarteners were ELs, compared with 7% of 8th and 9th graders in public schools as of Fall 2017). This pattern can tell educators that ELs in lower grades will be in middle and high school classrooms sooner or later. Although they may not be identified as ELs when they enter middle or high school, they are likely multilingual. It is safe to assume that approximately 20% of students in public middle and high school classrooms in the United States will be multilingual in the very near future. Researchers and practitioners must be prepared to work with and for adolescent multilingual students. This book can give readers in-depth understandings of who adolescent multilingual students are, what their experiences and challenges with writing and literacy look like, how they grow as literate beings, and how they negotiate multiple literacies and identities in their daily lives, among others. These discussions expand and deepen the perspectives of adolescent literacy.

Finally, I want to mention some contributions of this book specifically to the field of L2 writing. The discussions and syntheses of the literature in this book can raise researchers' and practitioners' attention to adolescent multilingual writing; this book illuminates a great variety of textual resources, activities, and experiences in which adolescent multilingual writers engage in their daily lives. Further, the discussions in this book can help L2 writing scholars move toward a model of adolescent multilingual writing. L2 writing scholars have long been interested in theory-building or building a model of L2 writing (e.g., Cumming, 1998; Grabe, 2001; Matsuda, 1998; Silva, 1993). Yet, there is no adequate theory or model of L2 writing that can explain how to learn to write in an L2 or multiple languages. Underscoring L2 writers' out-of-school literate lives and adopting a symbiotic approach to understanding multilingual writing can contribute to building a model of adolescent multilingual writing.

Furthermore, this book shows that empirical research, critical discussions, and comprehensive syntheses of L2 writing research can provide valuable insights into L1 writing and literacy studies. Typically, the L2 writing field has drawn upon theory and research in the L1 literacy field, thus, there have been conversations about how L2/multilingual writing research has been influenced by L1 studies. Yet, L2 writing scholars have rarely discussed ways in which L2/multilingual literacy research can influence and contribute to L1 literacy research. As pointed out earlier, the discussions on adolescent multilingual writing in this book can contribute to advancing theory, research, and pedagogy in L1 literacy, especially adolescent literacy, by expanding the perspectives of literacy and reconceptualizing adolescent multilingual writing and literacy. I believe that understandings and discussions about L2/multilingual students will become more critical for L1 literacy researchers and practitioners as more and more multilingual students are present in English-medium instructional contexts. This book engages L2 writing scholars in critical conversations about the broader implications of their work (e.g., thinking about to what extent and how L2 writing field can contribute to L1 literacy studies).

Future Directions

This book illustrates the complexity of adolescent multilingual writing across multiple contexts, underscoring the importance of out-of-school writing for students' literate lives. While proposing an expanded perspective, called a symbiotic approach, to the connections between in-school and out-of-school writing and literacy practices, this book aims to reconceptualize adolescent multilingual literacy. Discussions and arguments, as well as the syntheses of the literature in this book, can broaden the conversation of and research agenda for adolescent (multilingual) literacy. They also allow me to suggest theoretical, methodological, and pedagogical implications in this section.

Implications for Research

Syntheses of the research reveal how little research has been conducted on adolescent multilingual writing. Perhaps it is not surprising that the combination of three less popular or underexplored topics in literacy research, such as *adolescents, multilinguals,* and *writing,* has led to a research niche. In this sense, I welcome any kinds of studies on adolescent multilingual writers and writing. However, I make some suggestions for future research based on the discussions and research insights offered in previous chapters. All the suggestions are not necessarily limited to the implications for adolescent multilingual writers, but many of them can be applied to research on adolescent literacy.

I make some topical suggestions for future research. First, the use and role of *emerging technologies* seem to be one of the most significant issues in terms of examining and understanding adolescent (multilingual) literacy. In particular, studies surveyed about adolescent multilingual students' digital out-of-school writing in Chapter 3 indicate that online and digital spaces serve as a *contact zone* that incorporates multiple languages, literacies, identities, and cultures (e.g., native, host, transnational, online, and popular culture), as well as enables adolescent students to engage in rich, authentic, and interactive literacy practices. Therefore, it is worth examining the role that emerging technologies and online spaces (e.g., fan fiction communities and social networking communities) can play in adolescents' literate lives.

Second, issues of identity and literacy are especially compelling when researchers and practitioners work with and for adolescent students. Much of identity-literacy research has examined how adolescent students use writing to reflect who they are and negotiate their multiple identities. In other words, the focus of such research has been on the possibilities of writing practices for identity construction. Relatively little is known about how their identities actually influence their writing and literacy practices for academic and other purposes. To fill this gap, researchers can investigate the impact of adolescent students' identities, mostly multiple and conflicting, upon writing and literacy practices. For instance, researchers can ask how individual's identities influence the choices and opportunities around writing activities and events (e.g., types and topics of writing they prefer or avoid and what languages they use). For a comprehensive picture, researchers should investigate the bidirectional relationship between identity construction and literacy practices.

Third, adolescent multilingual students are asked to show their knowledge about what they learn in content area classrooms (e.g., social studies and science) through writing. Yet, studies have shown that adolescent ELs tend to engage in less challenging and smaller amounts of writing and literacy tasks in content area classrooms. Additionally, very few empirical studies have been conducted about adolescent multilingual students' writing practices in content area classrooms. Future research into the *intersection* of content area learning and writing development can explicate how writing practices can help students engage in content area learning and vice versa. Such research requires collaborative research between content area experts and writing/literacy researchers.

Fourth, it was quite shocking that I was not able to find much empirical research around adolescent multilingual writing for social impact. Existing research has demonstrated various purposes or functions of writing for adolescent multilingual students (e.g., writing to communicate, learn, explore identities, and express themselves). Yet, little research seems to address writing for civic engagement or writing for social action in multilingual contexts. Adolescent writing is not just for academic purposes, but it serves a wider range of functions. I would like to invite researchers and practitioners to explore and address writing for social impact and action.

Finally, the concepts of writing development and writing development research need to be revisited, and more empirical research on writing development is needed. Writing development research in the field of L2 writing tends to be limited to exploring the development of academic writing in English over a short period of time. Yet, researchers need to explore adolescent multilingual students' writing development in two or more languages, keeping multi-year trajectories of writing development in mind. Certainly, it will be time-consuming to explore how bi- and multilingual students develop L1 literacy, along with academic writing in English over longer stretches of time, but worth pursuing so as to better understand how multilingual students grow and change over time.

In addition to topical suggestions, I would like to make some suggestions related to adopting a symbiotic approach to research and pedagogy. One of the main arguments in this book is that researchers and practitioners should adopt a symbiotic approach to examining students' in-school and out-of-school literate lives to gain a more comprehensive understanding of the nature of adolescent writing and literacy. To achieve this, researchers need to examine (a) the role of out-of-school literacy in academic literacy learning, (b) the role of in-school literacy in out-of-school literate lives, and (c) the role of literacy learning in the future. In particular, writing practices and instruction in the classroom should help young people successfully use writing for personal well-being, entertainment, civic engagement, and more beyond regular school hours. Furthermore, writing practices in school should help our students learn how to navigate future literacy practices that we cannot even imagine or predict now. Given that, researchers should engage in more critical conversations and reflections on whether or not what students do with language and literacy in school really matters to their literate lives beyond the classroom and how. Furthermore, when researchers explore the interdependent and interrelated relationships between in-school and out-of-school writing and literacy practices, they should discuss the mutually beneficial and supportive relationships between the two, as well as tensions and contradictions between them that could negatively influence their literacy experiences, practices, and learning in general. Finally, researchers need to consider student perspectives about the relationships between in-school and out-of-school practices. In other words, it will be worth asking students' perceptions of how in-school literacy practices influence their out-of-school literate lives and vice versa. In addition, it is important to inquire about their sense of connecting the two for literacy learning and more.

Notwithstanding, I cannot overlook some of the methodological complexities inherent in researching adolescent (multilingual) literacy practices across various contexts. One of the challenges of conducting adolescent literacy research, especially outside of school, is that it is difficult to document students' writing and literacy practices through everyday living situations (Godwin-Jones, 2019, p. 457). Unlike classroom research that is conducted in one physical setting, out-of-school research, especially in online spaces, is not easy to observe and record because participants move across multiple settings so swiftly, and data (e.g., online texts) can be constantly updated, revised, or deleted (Warner, 2016). Similarly, an exploration into writing and literacy practices across multiple contexts can be extremely challenging and time-consuming if one researcher attempted to follow participants across diverse settings. To address these challenges, I suggest that researchers should consider inviting adolescent students as researchers themselves. The student-as-researcher method can be compelling enough to engage them in collaborative adolescent literacy research. For instance, Zenkov et al. (2014) conducted a youth participatory action study on writing instruction for diverse youth and English learners in a mid-Atlantic city in the United States. These authors were a team of teacher educators/university researchers and classroom teachers. While employing a "kids as researcher" method (p. 306), the research team invited participating adolescent ELs to document their own literacy practices. The participating students were given digital cameras with explicit instruction about some basics of camera operation. Each participant took an average of 100 pictures that they could use in order to respond to the three project questions (i.e., the purpose of school, supports for and impediments to school and literacy success). When students brought some pictures to the class, they examined, selected, and discussed them with the research team members. Then, together they produced some writing about their pictures. The kids-as-researchers method can generate data that researchers alone may not be able to obtain, explicitly invite students to share their literate lives across multiple contexts, and gain students' perspectives on adolescent literacy and school experiences.

Given the great potential and lack of adolescent multilingual writing research, I call for establishing adolescent multilingual writing as an emerging area of inquiry and an interdisciplinary genre. Writing well is a necessity for young people since writing is a critical 21st century skill and tool for educational, occupational, and social achievement. For adolescent multilingual students, writing plays a significant role in promoting L2 proficiency (Manchón & Cerezo, 2018; Williams, 2012), in facilitating their learning of subject matters (Hirvela, 2011; Hirvela, Hyland, & Manchón, 2016), and in exploring and expressing identities

(Black, 2009; Yi, 2013). Establishing adolescent multilingual writing as an emerging area of inquiry can yield more empirical research and help us work toward a model of adolescent multilingual writing, which will eventually enrich the field of L2 writing. Similarly, I suggest that L1 literacy scholars, especially adolescent literacy scholars seek to understand and explore adolescent *multilingual* students and their writing in adolescent literacy research. Beyond an English-monolingual perspective of exploring adolescent literacy, L1 literacy scholars should carve out a space for multilingual literacy research within literacy studies.

Implications for Pedagogy

In this section, I will make some specific suggestions for classroom teachers. First, they need to develop more expanded notions of writing and literacy. They should situate academic writing and literacy within the notion of multiple literacies and consider it in relation to other kinds of writing and literacy (e.g., out-of-school writing) (Villalva, 2006). Furthermore, they should acknowledge both academic and out-of-school writing and literacy as equally legitimate and meaningful to young people with each serving different functions or purposes in their lives. They also need to take a symbiotic approach to their writing and literacy pedagogy. In other words, while capitalizing on students' out-of-school experiences, resources, and knowledge for academic practices, they should critically think about how in-school writing and literacy learning can positively influence student' out-of-school literate lives now and later. With their critical reflection on the latter, teachers need to envision multiple kinds of literacy skills, knowledge, and literate identities that will be necessary for young people to be successful in life and society. Teachers should prepare our students for "what will be available in the future that we cannot anticipate or predict" (Chun, Kern, & Smith, 2016, p. 72). In this manner, students will be able to figure out how to learn and navigate new literacy practices.

When teachers hold these perspectives of writing and literacy, they can implement some innovative activities into classroom practices. For instance, instead of teaching only text-based academic writing and literacy in English, teachers can embrace more multilingual, multicultural, and multimodal writing and literacy practices. Teachers can also engage students in explicit conversations around questions, such as, "What are the similarities and differences between in-school and out-of-school writing and literacy practices?," "How do students negotiate tensions and contradictions between the two practices?" and

"How do their in-school writing and literacy learning influence their literate lives outside of school?" and so forth. Drawing upon critical conversations with students around these questions, teachers can create learning opportunities that recognize adolescent (multilingual) students as writers, leverage their rich literate experiences from varied contexts, and explore how their in-school learning prepares them for life outside of school.

Given that "literacy work is identity work." (Guzzetti & Gamboa, 2004, p. 413), writing pedagogy should aim to help students develop positive identities as writers so that they will actually write, enjoy writing, find the meaning of writing, and see the value of writing. Teachers can easily overlook this aspect of writing pedagogy as they are faced with standards, high-stakes testing, and rigid curricula. To achieve this goal, teachers can implement "inquiry-based" projects that are rooted in students' interests, strengths, and lived experiences (Enright, 2011, p. 113).

In conclusion, I have provided several specific directions for future research and pedagogy that emerge from discussions and research insights offered in the previous chapters in this book. Since this book focuses more on discussing the connections between in-school and out-of-school writing and literacy practices, there must be some important questions about adolescent multilingual writing that have not been fully explored here. I now invite the L2 writing and adolescent literacy communities to pay more attention to adolescent multilingual students and their literate lives as more rigorous research and critical dialogues about adolescent multilingual students will contribute to advancing the fields of L2 writing and adolescent literacy.

References

Black, R. W. (2009). Online fan fiction, global identities, and imagination. *Research in the Teaching of English*, *43*(4), 397–425.

Chun, D., Kern, R. & Smith, B. (2016). Technology in language use, language teaching, and language learning. *Modern Language Journal*, *100*(S1), 64–80. https://doi.org/10.1111/modl.12302

Condition of Education (2020, May 19). *The condition of education 2020*. National Center for Education Statistics. https://nces.ed.gov/pubsearch/pubsinfo.asp?pubid=2020144

Cumming, A. (1998). Theoretical perspectives on writing. *Annual Review of Applied Linguistics*, *18*, 61–78. https://doi.org/10.1017/S0267190500003482

Enright, K. A. (2011). Language and literacy for a new mainstream. *American Educational Research Journal*, *48*(1), 80–118. https://doi.org/10.3102/0002831210368989

Godwin-Jones, R. (2019). Future directions in informal language learning. In M. Dressman & R. W. Sadler (Eds.), *The handbook of informal language learning* (pp. 457–470). Hoboken, NJ: Wiley-Blackwell. https://doi.org/10.1002/9781119472384.ch30

Grabe, W. (2001). Notes toward a theory of second language writing. In T. Silva & P. K. Matsuda (Eds.), *On second language writing* (pp. 39–57). Mahwah, NJ: Erlbaum.

Guzzetti, B. J., & Gamboa, M. (2004). Zines for social justice: Adolescent girls writing on their own. *Reading Research Quarterly, 39*(4), 408–436. https://doi.org/10.1598/RRQ.39.4.4

Hirvela, A. (2011). Writing to learn in content area: Research insights. In R. M. Manchón (Ed.), *Learning-to-write and writing-to-learn in an additional language* (pp. 37–59). Amsterdam, the Netherlands: John Benjamins.

Hirvela, A., Hyland, K., & Manchón, R. (2016). Dimensions in L2 writing theory and research: Learning to write and writing to learn. In P. K. Matsuda & R. Manchón (Eds.), *Handbook of second and foreign language writing* (pp. 45–64). Berlin, Germany: De Gruyter Mouton. https://doi.org/10.1515/9781614511335-005

Manchón, R., & Cerezo, L. (2018). Writing as language learning. In J. I. Liontas (Ed.). *The TESOL encyclopedia of English language teaching*. Hoboken, NJ: Wiley Blackwell. https://doi.org/10.1002/9781118784235.eelt0530

Matsuda, P. K. (1998). Situating ESL writing in a cross-disciplinary context. *Written Communication, 15*(1), 99–121. https://doi.org/10.1177/0741088398015001004

Silva, T. (1993). Toward an understanding of the distinct nature of L2 writing: The ESL research and its implications. *TESOL Quarterly, 27*(4), 657–677. https://doi.org/10.2307/3587400

Villalva, K. E. (2006). Hidden literacies and inquiry approaches of bilingual high school writers. *Written Communication, 23*(1), 91–129. https://doi.org/10.1177/0741088305283929

Warner, J. (2016). Adolescents' dialogic composing with mobile phones. *Journal of Literacy Research, 48*(2), 164–191. https://doi.org/10.1177/1086296X16660655

Williams, J. (2012). The potential role(s) of writing in second language development. *Journal of Second Language Writing, 21*(4), 321–331. https://doi.org/10.1016/j.jslw.2012.09.007

Yi, Y. (2005). Asian adolescents' in and out-of-school encounters with English and Korean literacy. *Journal of Asian Pacific Communication, 15*(1), 57–77. https://doi.org/10.1075/japc.15.1.06yi

Yi, Y. (2013). Adolescent multilingual writer's negotiation of multiple identities and access to academic writing: A case study of a Jogi Yuhak student in a US high school. *Canadian Modern Language Review, 69*(2), 207–231. https://doi.org/101353/cml.2013.0017

Zenkov, K., Pellegrino, A., Sell, C., Ewaida, M., Bell, A., Fell, M., Biernesser, S., & McCamis, M. (2014). Picturing kids and "kids" as researchers: Preservice teachers and effective writing instruction for diverse youth and English language learners. *The New Educator, 10*(4), 306–330. https://doi.org/10.1080/1547688X.2014.965107

Index

For Product Safety Concerns and Information please contact our EU
representative GPSR@taylorandfrancis.com
Taylor & Francis Verlag GmbH, Kaufingerstraße 24, 80331 München, Germany

www.ingramcontent.com/pod-product-compliance
Ingram Content Group UK Ltd.
Pitfield, Milton Keynes, MK11 3LW, UK
UKHW021055080625
459435UK00003B/14